Practical Japanese

▶ Your Guide to Speaking Japanese Quickly and Effortlessly in a Few Hours

by Jun Maeda

TUTTLE Publishing

Tokyo | Rutland, Vermont | Singapore

ABOUT TUTTLE
"Books to Span the East and West"

Our core mission at Tuttle Publishing is to create books which bring people together one page at a time. Tuttle was founded in 1832 in the small New England town of Rutland, Vermont (USA). Our fundamental values remain as strong today as they were then—to publish best-in-class books informing the English-speaking world about the countries and peoples of Asia. The world has become a smaller place today and Asia's economic, cultural and political influence has expanded, yet the need for meaningful dialogue and information about this diverse region has never been greater. Since 1948, Tuttle has been a leader in publishing books on the cultures, arts, cuisines, languages and literatures of Asia. Our authors and photographers have won numerous awards and Tuttle has published thousands of books on subjects ranging from martial arts to paper crafts. We welcome you to explore the wealth of information available on Asia at **www.tuttlepublishing.com**.

Published by Tuttle Publishing, an imprint of Periplus Editions (HK) Ltd.

www.tuttlepublishing.com

Library of Congress Catalog No. 64-24949

ISBN 978-0-8048-4774-2

Previously published in 2004 as Let's Study Japanese ISBN: 0-8048-0362-5.

23 22 21 20 19
11 10 9 8 7
1908CM

Printed in China

TUTTLE PUBLISHING® is a registered trademark of Tuttle Publishing, a division of Periplus Editions (HK) Ltd.

Distributed by:

Japan
Tuttle Publishing
Yaekari Building 3rd Floor 5-4-12 Osaki
Shinagawa-ku, Tokyo 141-0032
Tel: (81)3 5437-0171; Fax: (81)3 5437-0755
sales@tuttle.co.jp
www.tuttle.co.jp

North America, Latin America & Europe
Tuttle Publishing
364 Innovation Drive
North Clarendon, VT 05759-9436
Tel: 1(802) 773-8930; Fax: 1(802) 773 6993
info@tuttlepublishing.com
www.tuttlepublishing.com

Asia Pacific
Berkeley Books Pte Ltd
3 Kallang Sector #04-01
Singapore 349278
Tel: (65) 6741-2178; Fax: (65) 6741-2179
inquiries@periplus.com.sg
www.periplus.com

Contents

Foreword

In this modern jet age, one can reach any part of the world within a day or less. Although English is widely spoken, it is very helpful to have some knowledge of the language of the country which you are visiting in order to make your trip more enjoyable by communicating with the local people and understanding their culture.

Intended for beginners who wish to learn to speak very basic Japanese in just a few hours, this book is written in a clear and simple yet versatile way. With approximately 350 basic words and examples of how they are used in practical conversational speech, one can acquire a fundamental working knowledge of Japanese from this book, so you can express yourself in simple Japanese sentences.

This book has several exercises for each lesson. And, to get acquainted with Japanese culture, the student may enjoy the photos which the author has provided as a visual aid. Complicated grammatical explanations are omitted, since detailed explanations sometimes discourage people from actually speaking. Only the essential points in pronunciation and grammar are given, and the phrases and the sentences are repeatedly presented in each lesson, so that the student can easily learn the phrases and practice using them without hesitancy or discouragement.

The author hopes that the tourist as well as the student or prospective foreign resident in Japan, young or old, may find this book a helpful and enjoyable tool in approaching the Japanese language for the first time.

Jun Maeda

A guide to pronunciation

There are five vowels in Japanese: **a**, **i**, **u**, **e**, **o**, all of which have both short and long sounds, as noted below. The long or "double" vowels are written with a macron (bar) over them. These vowels when used together with different consonants, make up new sounds. The consonants *c*, *l*, *q*, *v*, and *x* do not appear, although *ch* (as in *church*) does. The vowels are pronounced as follows (those that are doabled or have a line over them are longer):

ā	long **a**, pronounced *ah*, approximately as in *father*
a	same sound but shorter
ii	long **i**, pronounced *ee*, approximately as *ee* in *meet*
i	same sound but shorter
ū	long **u**, pronounced *oo*, approximately as oo in *root*
u	same sound but shorter, as *oo* in *wood*
ē	long **e**, pronounced *eh*, approximately as in *bed*
e	same sound but shorter
ō	long **o**, pronounced *oh*, approximately as in *tone*
o	same sound but shorter

Japanese consonants have virtually the same sounds as in English, except that the **g** is always hard (as in *get*) and the **r** is a sound between the English *r* and *l*. Double consonants, as in **jetto** (jet plane), **irasshaimase** (welcome, please come in), and **suitchi** (switch) must be pronounced clearly twice, just as in English "book-keeper" (double *k*) and "penknife" (double *n*). Each syllable in a Japanese word is in general pronounced distinctly, although in fairly rapid speech **i** and **u** are often shortened or omitted altogether, so that **desu** (am, is, are) sounds like **dess**, **deshita** (was, were) like **desh'ta**, and **arimasuka** (is there?, are there?) like **arimas'ka**. In this book therefore, the **i** and **u** are often omitted from the examples. The accent in Japanese is slight and almost monotonous. However, an emphasis in pitch and vowel length on particular syllables can often create a different meaning—e.g., **háshi** (chopsticks) and **hashi** (bridge), **kaki** (oyster) and **káki** (persimmon).

BASIC JAPANESE SOUNDS

Vowels	**a**	あ	**i**	い	**u**	う	**e**	え	**o**	お
	(ah)		**(ee)**		**(oo)**		**(eh)**		**(oh)**	
Consonants	**ka**	か	**ki**	き	**ku**	く	**ke**	け	**ko**	こ
+ vowels	**sa**	さ	**shi**	し	**su**	す	**se**	せ	**so**	そ
	ta	た	**chi**	ち	**tsu**	つ	**te**	て	**to**	と
	na	な	**ni**	に	**nu**	ぬ	**ne**	ね	**no**	の
	ha	は	**hi**	ひ	**fu**	ふ	**he**	へ	**ho**	ほ
	ma	ま	**mi**	み	**mu**	む	**me**	め	**mo**	も
	ya	や	**i**	い	**yu**	ゆ	**e**	え	**yo**	よ
	ra	ら	**ri**	り	**ru**	る	**re**	れ	**ro**	ろ
	wa	わ	**i**	い	**u**	う	**e**	え	**o**	お
	n	ん								
	ga	が	**gi**	ぎ	**gu**	ぐ	**ge**	げ	**go**	ご
	za	ざ	**ji**	じ	**zu**	ず	**ze**	ぜ	**zo**	ぞ
	da	だ	**ji**	じ	**zu**	ず	**de**	で	**do**	ど
	ba	ば	**bi**	び	**bu**	ぶ	**be**	べ	**bo**	ぼ
	pa	ぱ	**pi**	ぴ	**pu**	ぷ	**pe**	ぺ	**po**	ぽ
	kya	きゃ			**kyu**	きゅ			**kyo**	きょ
	sha	しゃ			**shu**	しゅ			**sho**	しょ
	cha	ちゃ			**chu**	ちゅ			**cho**	ちょ
	pya	ぴゃ			**pyu**	ぴゅ			**pyo**	ぴょ
	nya	にゃ			**nyu**	にゅ			**nyo**	にょ
	mya	みゃ			**myu**	みゅ			**myo**	みょ
	rya	りゃ			**ryu**	りゅ			**ryo**	りょ
	hya	ひゃ			**hyu**	ひゅ			**hyo**	ひょ
	gya	ぎゃ			**gyu**	ぎゅ			**gyo**	ぎょ
	bya	びゃ			**byu**	びゅ			**byo**	びょ
	ja	じゃ			**ju**	じゅ			**jo**	じょ

LESSON 1

What is this?

VOCABULARY

hai はい yes

iie いいえ no

nan, nani なん、なに what

sō そう so, exactly!

kore-wa これは this (or these)
NOTE: adding **-wa** at the end of a word emphasizes that it is the primary subject of the sentence.

de-wa arimasen では ありません is not, are not

dess-ka ですか is, are, am
NOTE: (The more formal and correct form is **desu-ka** but in everyday speech the **u** in **desu** is left out). Adding **-ka** at the end of a sentence is like adding a question mark and makes the sentence into a question.

hon 本 book

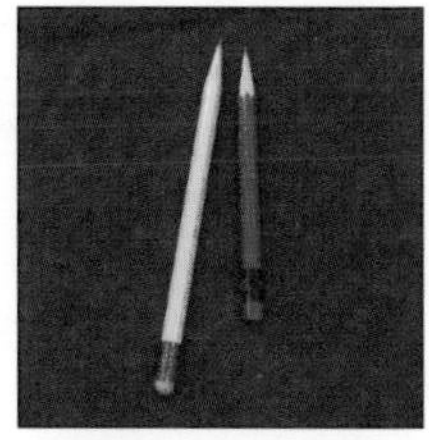
empitsu えんぴつ pencil

inu 犬 dog

hana 花 flower

jidōsha 自動車 car

hikōki 飛行機 airplane

kudamono くだもの
fruit

geta 下駄
wooden clogs

kutsu 靴 shoes

PHRASES

Kore-wa nan dess-ka? これは 何 ですか?
What is this? (literally: "This–what–is?")

Kore-wa hon dess. これは 本 です。
This is a book. (literally: "This–book–is.")

Kore-wa empitsu dess. これは えんぴつ です。
This is a pencil. (literally: "This–pencil–is.")

Kore-wa inu dess. これは 犬 です。
This is a dog. (literally: "This–dog–is.")

Kore-wa hana dess. これは 花 です。
This is a flower. (These are flowers.) (literally: "This–flower–is.")

Kore-wa jidōsha dess-ka? これは 自動車 ですか?
Is this a car? (Adding **-ka** at the end makes it a question.)
(literally: "This–car–is?")

Hai, sō dess. はい、そうです。 Yes, it is (exactly so).

Kore-wa hikōki dess-ka? これは 飛行機 ですか?
Is this an airplane? (literally: "This–airplane–is?")

Iie, sō de-wa arimasen. いいえ、そう では ありません。
No, it is not.

Kore-wa inu dess-ka? これは 犬 ですか? Is this a dog?

Iie, sō de-wa arimasen. いいえ、そう では ありません。
No, it is not.

Kore-wa hana dess-ka? これは 花 ですか?
Is this a flower? (Are these flowers?)

Iie, sō de-wa arimasen. Kore-wa kudamono dess.
いいえ、そう では ありません。 これは くだもの です。
No, it is not. (No, they are not.) This is a fruit.

Kore-wa kutsu dess-ka? これは 靴 ですか? Are these shoes?

Iie, kore-wa geta dess. いいえ、これは 下駄 です。
No, these are wooden clogs.

NOTE: In Japanese the same form of a noun or verb can be either singular or plural. The context usually makes clear what is meant. Occasionally, when it is necessary to be quite explicit, a pluralizing suffix can be added to nouns (and is frequently added to pronouns), but it is not essential for the beginner to be concerned about this usage now.

EXERCISES

Refer to the pictures on the right and fill in the blanks.

1. **Kore-wa ____________ dess.**
   This is a pencil.

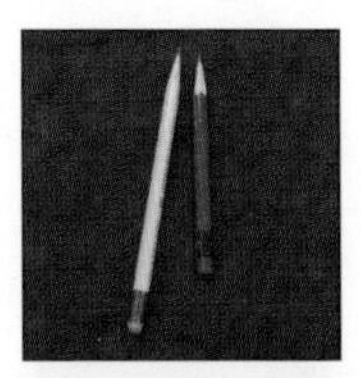

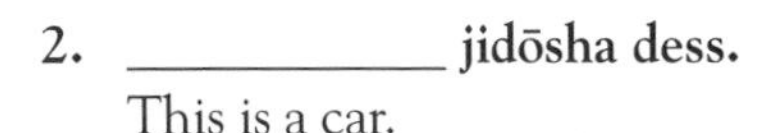

2. **____________ jidōsha dess.**
   This is a car.

3. **__________ __________ dess.**
This is a book.

4. **__________ __________ dess.**
This is a dog.

5. **Kore-wa hana dess-ka?**
Is this a flower?

Iie, kore-wa __________ dess.
No, this is a fruit.

6. **Kore-wa kudamono ____________ ?**
Is this a fruit?

Iie, kore-wa __________ dess.
No, this is a flower.

7. **Kore-wa jidōsha dess-ka?**
Is this a car?

Iie, sō de-wa __________ .
No, it is not.

Kore-wa __________ dess.
This is a airplane.

8. **Kore-wa geta dess-ka?**
Are these wooden clogs?

Iie, kore-wa __________ dess.
No, these are shoes.

LESSON 2

Where are you going?

VOCABULARY

koko ここ here

soko そこ there, over there

doko どこ where

-e へ to (a suffix indicating direction in the sense of "to")

arimahss あります is, are, there is, there are

ikimahss (or **yukimahss**) 行きます go, goes

watashi-wa 私は I
NOTE: The complete form is **watakshi-wa** but in everyday speech it is shortered to watashi-wa

anata-wa あなたは you (as the subject of a sentence)
NOTE: The suffix **-wa** indicates that the word it is attached to is the main subject of the sentence.

Tōkyō Eki 東京駅
Tokyo Station

uchi 家 home

hoteru ホテル
hotel

kūkō 空港 airport

nimotsu 荷物
luggage (or package)

shimbun 新聞
newspaper

kaisha 会社 office

heya 部屋 room

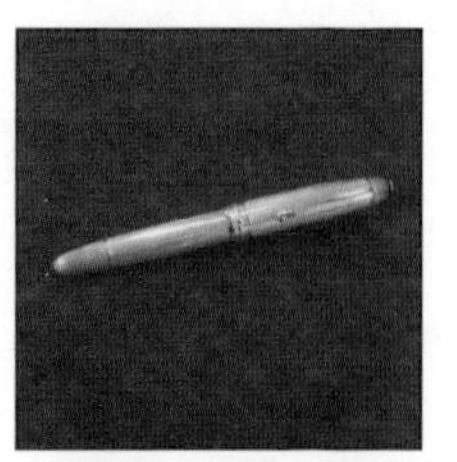

pen ペン pen

chikatetsu no eki
地下鉄の駅
subway station

resutoran
レストラン restaurant

basutei バス停
bus stop

PHRASES

Anata-wa doko-e ikimahss-ka (yukimahss-ka)?
あなたは　どこへ　行きますか?
Where are you going? (literally: "You where–to go?")

Watashi-wa Tōkyō Eki-e ikimahss. 私は　東京駅へ　行きます。
I am going to Tokyo Station. (literally: "I Tokyo Station–to go.")

Watashi-wa hoteru-e ikimahss. 私は　ホテルへ　行きます。
I am going to the hotel.

Watashi-wa uchi-e ikimahss. 私は　家へ　行きます。
I am going home.

Watashi-wa kūkō-e ikimahss. 私は　空港へ　行きます。
I am going to the airport.

Doko dess-ka? どこ　ですか? Where is it?

Koko dess. (Koko-ni arimahss.) ここ　です。(ここに　あります。)
Here it is. (Right here.)

Soko dess. (Soko-ni arimahss.) そこ　です。(そこに　あります。)
There it is. (Right over there.)

Nimotsu-wa doko dess-ka? 荷物は　どこ　ですか?
Where is the luggage (or package)? (literally: "Luggage–where–is–it?")

Shimbun-wa doko dess-ka? 新聞は　どこ　ですか?
Where is the newspaper?

Hoteru doko dess-ka? 部屋は　どこ　ですか?
Where is the hotel?

Pen-wa doko dess-ka? ペンは　どこ　ですか?
Where is the pen?

Basutei-wa doko dess-ka? バス停は　どこ　ですか?
Where is the bus stop?

EXERCISES

Refer to the pictures on the right and fill in the blanks.

1. **Watashi-wa __________ ikimahss.**
   I am going home.

2. **Watashi-wa __________ ikimahss.**
   I am going to Tokyo Station.

3. **Watashi-wa __________ ikimahss.**
   I am going to the hotel.

4. **Pen-wa ________ dess-ka?**
Where is the pen?

__________ dess.
It is here.

5. **Nimotsu-wa doko ________?**
Where is the luggage?

__________ dess.
There it is.

6. **____________ doko dess-ka?**
Where is the room?

__________ dess.
Here it is.

7. **Shimbun-wa ________ dess-ka?**
Where is the newspaper?

Soko __________ .
Here it is.

8. **Watashi-wa __________ ikimahss.**
I am going to the subway station.

9. **Watashi-wa __________ ikimahss.**
I am going to my office.

10. **____________ doko dess-ka?**
Where is the restaurant?

LESSON 3

Can you do it?

VOCABULARY

piano ピアノ piano

gorufu ゴルフ golf

Nihon 日本 Japan

-o を (suffix to indicate that a word is the object of the sentence)

iku-koto 行くこと going, to go (noun form)

kuru-koto 来ること coming, to come (noun form)

dekimahss できます to be able, can (speak, read, write, etc.)

dekimasen できません not able to, cannot (speak, read, write, etc.)

-ga が (suffix to indicate when a word is secondary the subject of a sentence)

Nihon ryōri 日本料理 Japanese food (dishes, cooking)

Eigo 英語 English

Nihongo 日本語 Japanese

ryōri 料理 food, cooking

yomu-koto 読むこと reading

kaku-koto 書くこと writing

taberu-koto 食べること eating

PHRASES

Anata-wa dekimahss-ka? あなたは　できますか?
Are you able (to speak, read, write, etc.)? Can you (do it)?

Hai, dekimahss. はい　できます。 Yes, I can.

Iie, dekimasen. いいえ　できません。 No, I can't.

Anata-wa Eigo-ga dekimahss-ka? あなたは　英語が　できますか?
Can you speak English? (literally: "You–English–can?")

Anata-wa Nihongo-ga dekimahss-ka?
あなたは　日本語が　できますか? Can you speak Japanese?

Anata-wa ryōri-ga dekimahss-ka? あなたは　料理が　できますか?
Can you cook? (literally: "You–cooking–can?")

Anata-wa yomu-koto-ga dekimahss-ka?
あなたは　読むことが　できますか? Can you read?

Anata-wa Nihongo-o kaku-koto-ga dekimahss-ka?
あなたは　日本語を　書くことが　できますか?
Can you write Japanese? (literally: "You–Japanese–writing–can?")

Anata-wa Nihon ryōri-o taberu-koto-ga dekimahss-ka?
あなたは　日本料理を　食べることが　できますか?
Can you eat Japanese food? (literally: "You–Japanese–food–eating–can?")

EXERCISES

Answer the question in Japanese.

1. **Anata-wa Eigo-ga dekimahss-ka?** Can you speak English?

   ___________, ___________. Yes, I can.

2. **Anata-wa Nihongo-ga dekimahss-ka?** Can you speak Japanese?

   ___________, ___________. No, I can't.

3. **Anata-wa gorufu-ga dekimahss-ka?** Can you play golf?

 ___________, ___________. Yes, I can.

4. **Anata-wa piano-ga ______________?** Can you play the piano?

 ___________, ___________. No, I cannot.

5. **Anata-wa Nihongo-o yomu-koto-ga dekimahss-ka?**
 Can you read Japanese?

 ___________, ___________. No, I can't.

6. ___________ **Eigo-o kaku-koto-ga dekimahss-ka?**
 Can you write English?

 ___________, ___________. Yes, I can.

7. **Anata-wa Nihon ryōri-o taberu-koto-ga dekimahss-ka?**
 Can you eat Japanese food?

 ___________, ___________. Yes, I can.

8. **Anata-wa Nihon-e iku-koto-ga dekimahss-ka?**
 Can you go to Japan?

 ___________, ___________. Yes, I can.

9. **Anata-wa uchi-e kuru-koto-ga dekimahss-ka?**
 Can you come home?

 ___________, ___________. No, I cannot.

10. **Anata-wa hoteru-e iku-koto-ga dekimahss-ka?**
 Can you go to the hotel?

 ___________, ___________. Yes, I can.

LESSON 4

Do you have it?

VOCABULARY

motte-imahss 持っています。
to have, possess

motte-imasen 持っていません。
haven't, don't have

kippu 切符 ticket

tokei 時計 watch

bōshi 帽子 hat

keitai denwa
携帯電話 cell phone

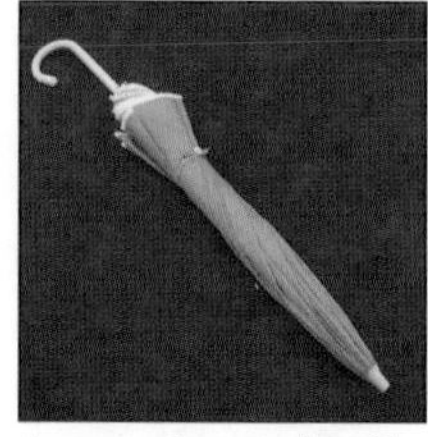

kasa 傘 umbrella

uwagi 上着
jacket (coat)

PHRASES

Anata-wa X-o motte-imahss-ka? あなたは Xを 持っていますか?
Do you have X?

Hai, motte-imahss. はい、持っています。 Yes, I have.

Iie, motte-imasen. いいえ、持っていません。 No, I don't have.

Anata-wa kippu-o motte-imahss-ka?
あなたは　切符を　持っていますか?
Do you have a ticket? (literally: "You–ticket–have?")

Anata-wa tokei-o motte-imahss-ka?
あなたは　時計を　持っていますか?
Do you have a watch (clock)?

Anata-wa bōshi-o motte-imahss-ka?
あなたは　帽子を　持っていますか?　Do you have a hat?

Anata-wa keitai denwa motte-imahss-ka?
あなたは　携帯電話を　持っていますか?
Do you have a cell phone?

Anata-wa kasa-o motte-imahss-ka?
あなたは　傘を　持っていますか?　Do you have an umbrella?

EXERCISES

Refer to the pictures on the right and fill in the blanks.

1. **Anata-wa kasa-o motte-imahss-ka?**
   Do you have an umbrella?

   Hai, __________.
   Yes, I have.

2. **Anata-wa tokei-o __________?**
   Do you have a watch?

   Hai, __________.
   Yes, I have.

3. **__________ keitai denwa-o motte-imahss-ka?**
   Do you have a cell phone?

   Iie, __________.
   No, I don't

4. **Anata-wa pen-o ________________?**
Do you have a pen?

__________ __________.
Yes, I have.

5. **__________ bōshi-o motte-imahss-ka?**
Do you have a hat?

__________ __________.
No, I don't.

6. **Anata-wa __________ motte-imahss-ka?**
Do you have a ticket?

__________ __________.
Yes, I have.

7. **Anata-wa keitai denwa-o ________________?**
Do you have a cell phone?

__________ __________.
Yes, I have.

8. **Anata-wa ________ motte-imahss-ka?**
Do you have an umbrella?

__________ __________.
No, I don't.

9. **Anata-wa uwagi-o________________?**
Do you have a jacket (coat)?

LESSON 5

Do you like it?

VOCABULARY

suki 好き like, likes

kirai 嫌い dislike, dislikes

ongaku 音楽
music

sushi すし sushi

gohan ご飯 rice

soba そば
noodles

sake 酒 sake

o-cha お茶
Japanese tea

kōhii コーヒー
coffee

shinkansen 新幹線
bullet train

sashimi 刺身
sashimi

PHRASES

Anata-wa X-ga suki dess-ka? あなたはＸが　好き　ですか?
Do you like X? (literally: "You–X–like?")

Hai, suki dess. はい、好き　です。
Yes, I do. (literally: "Yes–I–like–it.")

Iie, suki de-wa arimasen. いいえ、好き　では　ありません。
No, I don't. (literally: "No,–like–is–not.")

Kirai dess. 嫌い　です。 I dislike it. (literally: "Dislike–is.")

Anata-wa soba-ga suki dess-ka?
あなたは　そばが　好き　ですか?　Do you like noodles?

Anata-wa ongaku-ga suki dess-ka?
あなたは　音楽が　好き　ですか?
Do you like music? (literally: "You–music–like–is–it?")

Anata-wa sushi-ga suki dess-ka?
あなたは　すしが　好き　ですか?　Do you like sushi?

Anata-wa sake-ga suki dess-ka?
あなたは　酒が　好き　ですか?　Do you like sake?

EXERCISES

Answer the questions.

1. **Anata-wa gohan-ga suki dess-ka?**
   Do you like cooked rice?
   ________ ________ ________ .

2. **Anata-wa sushi-ga suki dess-ka?**
   Do you like sushi?
   ________ ________ ________ .

3. **Anata-wa soba-ga suki dess-ka?**
   Do you like noodles?

   ________ ________ ________ .

4. **Anata-wa kōhii-ga suki dess-ka?**
   Do you like coffee?

   ________ ________ ________ .

5. **Anata-wa shinkansen-ga suki dess-ka?**
   Do you like bullet train?

   ________ ________ ________ .

6. **Anata-wa o-cha-ga suki dess-ka?**
   Do you like (Japanese) tea?

   ________ ________ ________ .

7. **Anata-wa ongaku-ga suki dess-ka?**
   Do you like music?

   ________ ________ ________ .

8. **Anata-wa sashimi-ga suki dess-ka?**
   Do you like sashimi?

   ________ ________ ________ .

9. **Anata-wa sake-ga suki dess-ka?**
   Do you like sake?

   ________ ________ ________ .

LESSON 6

Please and thank you

VOCABULARY

dōzo どうぞ please

wata(k)shi-ni 私に to me

-ni に to, for, at, in (objective postposition)

...kudasai …ください (please) give me

dōmo どうも very, very much

sumimasen (suimasen) すみません（すいません） sorry, Thank you.

arigatō-gozaimahss. ありがとうございます Thank you.

arigatō (less formal) ありがとう Thank you.

o-mizu お水 water

supūn スプーン spoon

isu 椅子 chair

kami 紙 paper

haizara 灰皿 ashtray

tabako たばこ cigarette

raitā ライター
lighter

fōku フォーク
fork

napukin ナプキン
napkin

PHRASES

Dōzo watashi-ni X-o kudasai. どうぞ　私に　Xを　ください。
Please give me X.

Dōzo watashi-ni o-mizu-o kudasai.
どうぞ　私に　お水を　ください。
Please give me some (a drink of) water.

Dōzo watashi-ni supūn-o kudasai.
どうぞ　私に　スプーンを　ください。 Please give me a spoon.

Dōzo watashi-ni isu-o kudasai.
どうぞ　私に　椅子を　ください。 Please give me a chair.

Dōzo watashi-ni kami-o kudasai. どうぞ　私に　紙を　ください。
Please give me some paper.

Dōzo watashi-ni tabako-o kudasai.
どうぞ　私に　たばこを　ください。 Please give me a cigarette.

Arigatō-gozaimahss. ありがとうございます。 Thank you.

Dōmo arigatō-gozaimahss. どうも　ありがとうございます。
Thank you very much.

Dōmo sumimasen (suimasen). どうも　すみません（すいません）。
Thank you very much. (sometimes it means I'm sorry.)

EXERCISES

Refer to the pictures and fill in the blanks.

1. **Dōzo watashi-ni __________ kudasai.**
   Please give me a lighter.

   Arigatō-gozaimahss.
   Thank you very much.

2. **Dōzo __________ __________.**
   Please give me a napkin.

   Arigatō-gozaimahss.
   Thank you very much.

3. **Dōzo watashi-ni __________ kudasai.**
   Please give me a fork.

   Arigatō-gozaimahss.
   Thank you very much.

4. **Dōzo watashi-ni ____________________ .**
   Please give me a cigarette.

   ____________________ .
   Thank you very much.

5. **Dōzo watashi-ni __________ kudasai.**
   Please give me an ashtray.

   Dōmo ____________________ .
   Thank you very much.

6. **Dōzo __________ __________ kudasai.**
   Please give me some water.

   Dōmo ____________________ .
   Thank you very much.

LESSON 7

Numbers

VOCABULARY

1 **ichi, hitotsu** 一、一つ

2 **ni, futatsu** 二、二つ

3 **san, mittsu** 三、三つ

4 **shi, yon, yottsu** 四、四つ

5 **go, itsutsu** 五、五つ

6 **roku, muttsu** 六、六つ

7 **shichi, nana, nanatsu** 七、七つ

8 **hachi, yattsu** 八、八つ

9 **ku, kyū, kokonotsu** 九、九つ

10 **jū, tō** 十

NOTE : In the numbers from 1 through 10, the second word given in each case is the number used in referring to specfic things—e.g., **bōshi hitotsu** or **hitotsu-no bōshi** (one hat), **isu futatsu** or **futatsu-no isu** (two chairs), etc.

11 **jū-ichi** 十一

12 **jū-ni** 十二

13 **jū-san** 十三

14 **jū-shi, jū-yon** 十四

15 **jū-go** 十五

16 **jū-roku** 十六

17 **jū-shichi, jū-nana** 十七

18 **jū-hachi** 十八

19 **jū-ku, jū-kyū** 十九

20 **ni-jū** 二十

21 **ni-jū-ichi** 二十一

30 **san-jū** 三十

40 **shi-jū, yon-jū** 四十

50 **go-jū** 五十

60 **roku-jū** 六十

70 **nana-jū, shichi-jū** 七十

80 **hachi-jū** 八十

90 **kyū-jū** 九十

100 **hyaku** 百

101 **hyaku-ichi** 百一

150 **hyaku-go-jū** 百五十

200 **ni-hyaku** 二百

300 **sambyaku**
(**n-h** becomes **mb**) 三百

400 **yon-hyaku** 四百

500 **go-hyaku** 五百

600 **roppyaku**
(**ku+h** becomes **pp**) 六百

700 **nana-hyaku** 七百

800 **happyaku**
(**chi+h** becomes **pp**) 八百

900 **kyū-hyaku** 九百

1000 **sen** 千

5000 **go-sen** 五千

10000 **ichi-man** 一万

30000 **samman**
(**n-m** becomes **mm**) 三万

100,000 **jū-man** 十万

1,000,000 **hyaku-man** 百万

In counting people, the numbers are used as follows:

hitori 一人 one person

futari 二人 two persons, two people

san-nin 三人 three people

yo-nin 四人 four people

go-nin 五人 five people

roku-nin 六人 six people

shichi-nin, nana-nin 七人 seven people

hachi-nin 八人 eight people

ku-nin, kyū-nin 九人 nine people

jū-nin 十人 ten people

From 10 on, the suffix **–nin** is added to the number as given in the first table above, except that **yo** is always used instead of **shi** for 4 in counting people; hence **ni-jū-yo-nin**: 24 people.

EXERCISES

Read those numbers in Japanese.

1	__________	2	__________	3	__________
4	__________	5	__________	6	__________
7	__________	8	__________	9	__________
10	__________	20	__________	55	__________
70	__________	93	__________	100	__________
120	__________	350	__________	510	__________
600	__________	650	__________	700	__________
830	__________	900	__________	980	__________
1000	__________	1500	__________	1950	__________
1964	__________	5000	__________	10000	__________

Counting those numbers in Japanese.

1 (one)	_______________	一つ
2 (two)	_______________	二つ
3 (three)	_______________	三つ
4 (four)	_______________	四つ
5 (five)	_______________	五つ
6 (six)	_______________	六つ
7 (seven)	_______________	七つ
8 (eight)	_______________	八つ
9 (nine)	_______________	九つ
10 (ten)	_______________	十

LESSON 8

What time is it?

VOCABULARY

nan-ji 何時 what time

-ji 時 hours, o'clock

ichi-ji 1時 one o'clock

yo-ji (**yo**, not **shi**, in telling time) 4時 four o'clock

han 半 half, half past

fun (pun) 分 minute

ippun (**chi+f** becomes **pp**) 1分 one minute

ni-fun 2分 two minutes

sampun (**n+f** becomes **mp**) 3分 three minutes

yompun (**n+f** becomes **mp**) 4分 four minutes

go-fun 5分 five minutes

roppun (**ku+f** becomes **pp**) 6分 six minutes

nana-fun 7分 seven minutes

hachi-fun, happun 8分 eight minutes

kyū-fun 9分 nine minutes

juppun (**u+f** becomes **upp**) 10分 ten minutes

jū-go-fun 15分 fifteen minutes

ni-juppun 20分 twenty minutes

san-juppun 30分 thirty minutes

sugi 過ぎ after, past (in telling time)

mae 前 before, to (in telling time)

EXERCISES

Tell the time in Japanese?

Ichi-ji dess. It's one o'clock.	____________ It's three o'clock.	____________ It's six o'clock.
Yo-ji-han dess. It's half past four.	____________ It's seven-thirty.	____________ It's half past ten.
Ichi-ji jū-go-fun sugi dess. A quarter past one	____________ A quarter past eight	____________ A quarter past eleven
Ichi-ji jū-go-fun mae dess. A quarter to one	____________ A quarter to five	____________ A quarter to eight

Draw clock hands referring to the time.

LESSON 9

What day is it?

VOCABULARY

kyō 今日 today

nan 何 what?

nichi 日 day (of the month)

kinō 昨日 yesterday

deshita でした was, were

asu, ashita 明日 tomorrow

yōbi 曜日 day of the week

shū 週 week

konshū 今週 this week

senshū 先週 last week

raishū 来週 next week

kyūjitsu 休日 holiday

Tsuki 月 Month

S	M	T	W	T	F	S
1	2	3	4	5	6	7
8	9	10	11	12	13	14
15	16	17	18	19	20	21
22	23	24	25	26	27	28
29	30	31				

Shū 週 week

日	月	火	水	木	金	土
1	2	3	4	5	6	7

日	**Nichi-yōbi**	Sunday
月	**Getsu-yōbi**	Monday
火	**Ka-yōbi**	Tuesday
水	**Sui-yōbi**	Wednesday
木	**Moku-yōbi**	Thursday
金	**Kin-yōbi**	Friday
土	**Do-yōbi**	Saturday
休日	**Kyūjitsu**	Holiday

PHRASES

Kyō-wa nan nichi dess-ka? 今日は 何日 ですか?
What day of the month is it today?

Kyō-wa X nichi dess. 今日は X日 です。Today is the X.

Kyō-wa jū-roku nichi dess. 今日は 16日 です。
Today is the sixteenth.

Kinō-wa nan nichi deshita-ka? 昨日は 何日 でしたか?
What day of the month was it yesterday?

Kinō-wa jū-go nichi deshita. 昨日は 15日 でした。
Yesterday was the fifteenth.

Asu-wa (ashita-wa) nan nichi dess-ka? 明日は 何日 ですか?
What day of the month is it tomorrow?

Asu-wa jū-shichi nichi dess. 明日は 17日 です。
Tomorrow is the seventeenth.

DATES:

tsuitachi 1日（ついたち）
the first

futsuka 2日（ふつか）
the second

mikka 3日（みっか） the third

yokka 4日（よっか） the fourth

itsuka 5日（いつか） the fifth

muika 6日（むいか） the sixth

nanoka 7日（なのか）
the seventh

yōka 8日（ようか） the eighth

kokonoka 9日（ここのか）
the ninth

tōka 10日（とおか） the tenth

jū-ichi nichi 11日（じゅういちにち） the eleventh

jū-ni nichi 12日（じゅうににち）
the twelfth

jū-san nichi 13日（じゅうさんにち） the thirteenth

jū-yokka 14日（じゅうよっか）
the fourteenth

jū-go nichi 15日 the fifteenth

jū-roku nichi 16日
the sixteenth

jū-shichi nichi 17日
the seventeenth

jū-hachi nichi 18日
the eighteenth

jū-ku nichi 19日
the nineteenth

hatsuka 20日（はつか）
the twentieth

ni-jū-ichi nichi 21日
the twenty-first

ni-jū-ni nichi 22日
the twenty-second

ni-jū-san nichi 23日
the twenty-third

ni-jū-yokka 24日
the twenty-fourth

ni-jū-go nichi 25日
the twenty-fifth

ni-jū-roku nichi 26日
the twenty-sixth

ni-jū-shichi nichi 27日
the twenty-seventh

ni-jū-hachi nichi 28日
the twenty-eighth

ni-jū-ku nichi 29日
the twenty-ninth

san-jū nichi 30日
the thirtieth

san-jū-ichi nichi 31日
the thirty-first

PHRASES

Kyō-wa nan yōbi dess-ka? 今日は　何曜日　ですか?
What day of the week is it today?

Kyō-wa Getsu-yōbi dess. 今日は　月曜日　です。
Today is Monday.

Kinō-wa nan yōbi deshita-ka? 昨日は　何曜日　でしたか?
What day of the week was it yesterday?

Kinō-wa Nichi-yōbi deshita. 昨日は　日曜日　でした。
Yesterday was Sunday.

Asu-wa nan yōbi dess-ka? 明日は　何曜日　ですか?
What day of the week is it tomorrow?

Asu-wa Ka-yōbi dess. 明日は　火曜日　です。
Tomorrow is Tuesday.

EXERCISES

Refer to the calender on the above and fill in the blanks.

S	M	T	W	T	F	S
1	2	3	4	5	6	7
8	9	10	11	12	13	14

↑ **today**

1. **Nan nichi dess-ka?** What is the date?

   Kyō-wa ___________ dess. It's the twelfth.
   Kinō-wa ____________ deshita. Asu-wa ___________ dess.
   Yesterday was the eleventh. Tomorrow is the thirteenth.

日	月	火	水	木	金	土
1	2	3	4	5	6	7

↑ **today**

2. **Nan yōbi dess-ka?** What day of the week is it?

Kyō-wa ______________ **dess.** Today is Tuesday.
Kinō-wa ______________ **deshita.** Yesterday was Monday.
Asu-wa ______________ **dess.** Tomorrow is Wednesday.

S	M	T	W	T	F	S
1	2	3	4	5	6	7
8	9	10	11	12	13	14
15	16	17	18	19	20	21
22	23	24	25	26	27	28

↑ **today**

3. **Nan nichi dess-ka?** What is the date?

__________ **ni-jū-shichi nichi dess.** It's the twenty-seventh.
__________ **ni-jū-roku nichi deshita.**
Yesterday was the twenty-sixth.
__________ **ni-jū-hachi nichi dess.**
Tomorrow is the twenty-eighth.

4. **Nan yōbi dess-ka?** What day of the week is it?

Kyō-wa ______________ **dess.** Today is Friday.
Kinō-wa ______________ **deshita.** Yesterday was Thursday.
Asu-wa ______________ **dess.** Tomorrow is Saturday.

日	月	火	水	木	金	土
1	2	3	4	5	6	7
8	9	10	11	12	13	14

← today

5. **Nan nichi dess-ka?** What is the date?

   Kyō-wa ________________ **dess.** It's the seventh.
   Ashita-wa ______________ **dess.** Tomorrow is the eighth.

6. **Nan yōbi dess-ka?** What day of the week is it?

   Kyō-wa ________________ **dess.** It is Saturday.
   Ashita-wa ______________ **dess.** Tomorrow is Sunday.

S	M	T	W	T	F	S
1	2	3	4	5	6	7
8	9	10	11	12	13	14

7. **Nan nichi dess-ka?** What is the date?

   Kyo-wa tō-ka dess. It's the tenth.
   Kinō-wa __________ **deshita.**
   Yesterday was the nineth.
   Ashita-wa __________ **dess.**
   Tomorrow is the eleventh.

8. **Nan yōbi dess-ka?** What day of the week is it?

   Kyō-wa ka-yōbi dess. Today is Tuesday.
   Kinō-wa ______________ **deshita.** Yesterday was Monday.
   Asu-wa ______________ **dess.** Tomorrow is Wednesday.

LESSON 10

Seasons and months

VOCABULARY

kikō 気候 climate

ikaga いかが how

atatakai 暖かい warm

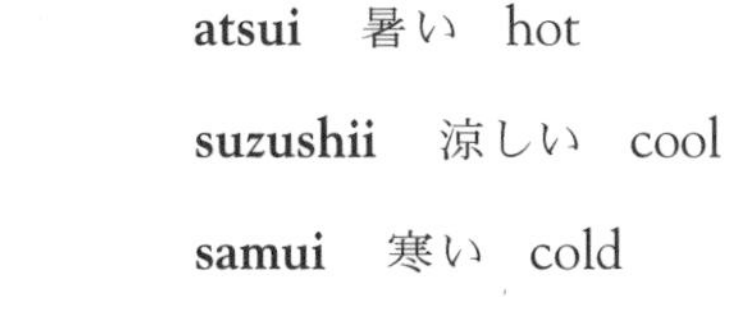

atsui 暑い hot

suzushii 涼しい cool

samui 寒い cold

haru: 春 spring:

San-gatsu 三月 March

Shi-gatsu 四月 April

Go-gatsu 五月 May

natsu: 夏 summer:

Roku-gatsu 六月 June

Shichi-gatsu 七月 July

Hachi-gatsu 八月 August

aki: 秋 autumn:

Ku-gatsu 九月 September

Jū-gatsu 十月 October

Jū-ichi-gatsu 十一月 November

fuyu: 冬 winter:

Jū-ni-gatsu 十二月 December

Ichi-gatsu 一月 January

Ni-gatsu 二月 February

kongetsu 今月 this month **sengetsu** 先月 last month

raigetsu 来月 next month

NOTE: The word "month" is expressed in three ways in Japanese: **tsuki**, -**getsu**, and -**gatsu**, the last two being used only as suffixes. In giving the number of months (one month, two months, etc.), the easiest system for the beginner is as follows:

ikkagetsu 1か月 one month

nikagetsu 2か月 two months

sankagetsu 3か月 three months

yonkagetsu 4か月 four months

gokagetsu 5か月 five months

rokkagetsu 6か月 six months

nanakagetsu 7か月 seven months

hachikagetsu, hakkagetsu 8か月 eight months

kyūkagetsu 9か月 nine months

jukkagetsu 10か月 ten months

jū-ikkagetsu 11か月 eleven months

jū-nikagetsu 12か月 twelve months

PHRASES

Kikō-wa dō dess-ka? 気候は どう ですか?
How is the climate? (What is the climate like?)

Haru-wa atatakai dess. 春は 暖かい です。
Spring is warm. (It is warm in spring.)

Natsu-wa atsui dess. 夏は　暑い　です。
Summer is hot. (It is hot in summer.)

Aki-wa suzushii dess. 秋は　涼しい　です。
Autumn is cool. (It is cool in autumn.)

Fuyu-wa samui dess. 冬は　寒い　です。
Winter is cold. (It is cold in winter.)

EXERCISES

1. Fill in the blanks:

Fuyu-wa ________________ dess.
Winter is cold. (It is cold in winter.)

Natsu-wa ________________ dess.
Summer is hot. (It is hot in summer.)

Aki-wa ________________ dess.
Autumn is cool. (It is cool in autumn.)

Haru-wa ________________ dess.
Spring is warm. (It is warm in spring.)

2. Draw am arrow to the correct month:

Go-gatsu 五月 ⟶	May
Ichi-gatsu 一月	August
Roku-gatsu 六月	December
Hachi-gatsu 八月	June
Jū-ni-gatsu 十二月	January
Ku-gatsu 九月	February
Jū-gatsu 十月	April
Jū-ichi-gatsu 十一月	November
Ni-gatsu 二月	July
Shi-gatsu 四月	October
Shichi-gatsu 七月	September

LESSON 11

Greetings and expressions

VOCABULARY

isha 医者 doctor

namae 名前 name

jūsho 住所 address

sensei 先生 teacher

gakusei 学生 student

anata-no あなたの your

Sayōnara. さようなら。 Goodbye.

bijiness-man ビジネスマン businessman

Amerika-jin アメリカ人 an American, American people

Igirisu-jin イギリス人 a British, British people

Furansu-jin フランス人 a French, French people

Doitsu-jin ドイツ人 a German, German people

Nihon-jin 日本人 a Japanese, Japanese people

Chūgoku-jin 中国人 a Chinese, Chinese people

Omedetō-gozaimahss. おめでとうございます。 Congratulations!

Irasshaimase. いらっしゃいませ。 Welcome. Please come in.

Gomen-nasai. ごめんなさい。 I am sorry. (Excuse me, Pardon me.)

Oyasumi-nasai. おやすみなさい。Good night.

Komban-wa. こんばんは。 Good evening.

Ohayō-gozaimahss. おはようございます。 Good morning.

Konnichi-wa. こんにちは。 Good day. (Hello. Good afternoon.)

Itadakimahss. いただきます。 I shall (eat)., Let's eat. (This expression is used before eating, to invite all present to eat)

Gochisō-sama. ごちそうさま。 (This expression is used after eating. It means something like "It was delicious" or "It was a treat.")

PHRASES

Anata-no namae-wa nan dess-ka?
あなたの　名前は　何　ですか?　What is your name?

Anata-wa X dess-ka?　あなたは　X　ですか?　Are you a (an) X?

Hai, sō dess.　はい、そう　です。 Yes, I am.

Iie, watashi-wa X dess.　いいえ、私は　X　です。
No, I am a (an) X.

Anata-wa Amerika-jin dess-ka?　あなたは　アメリカ人　ですか?
Are you American?

Anata-wa Igirisu-jin dess-ka?　あなたは　イギリス人　ですか?
Are you British?

Anata-wa Furansu-jin dess-ka?　あなたは　フランス人　ですか?
Are you French?

Anata-wa Nihon-jin dess-ka?　あなたは　日本人　ですか?
Are you Japanese?

Anata-wa isha dess-ka?　あなたは　医者　ですか?
Are you a doctor?

Anata-wa sensei dess-ka?　あなたは　先生　ですか?
Are you a teacher?

Iie, watashi-wa bijiness-man dess.
いいえ、私は　ビジネスマン　です。 No, I am a businessman.

Anata-wa gakusei dess-ka?　あなたは　学生　ですか?
Are you a student?

Iie, watashi-wa sensei dess.　いいえ、私は　先生　です。
No, I am a teacher.

Anata-no jūsho-o oshiete kudasai.
あなたの　住所を　教えて　ください。 Please give me your address.

EXERCISES

Answer the question.

1. **Anata-wa isha dess-ka?**
   Are you a doctor?

   Hai, watashi-wa ________ dess.
   Yes, I am a doctor.

2. **Anata-wa sensei dess-ka?**
   Are you a teacher?

   Hai, ________ ________ dess.
   Yes, I am a teacher.

3. **Anata-wa gakusei dess-ka?**
   Are you a student?

   ________ ________ bijiness-man dess.
   No, I am a busiessman.

4. **Anata-wa sensei dess-ka?**
   Are you a teacher?

   ________ ________ gakusei dess.
   No, I am a student.

5. **Anata-wa isha dess-ka?**
   Are you a doctor?

   ________ ________ sensei dess.
   No, I am a teacher.

6. **Anata-wa Igirisu-jin dess-ka?**
   Are you a British?

   ________ ________ Fransu-jin dess.
   No, I am a French.

7. **Anata-wa Amerika-jin dess-ka?**
   Are you an American?

   ________ ________ Doitsu-jin dess.
   No, I am a German.

LESSON 12

Food and eating

VOCABULARY

tabemono 食べ物 food

shinsen 新鮮 fresh

oishii おいしい tasty, delicious

shiroi 白い white

akai 赤い red

yawarakai やわらかい soft

katai 硬い hard, crisp

marui 丸い round

shikakui 四角い square

amai 甘い sweet

karai 辛い salty

tsumetai 冷たい cold, cool

atsui 熱い hot

nagai 長い long

omeshi-agari kudasai. お召し上がり ください。 Please help yourself. (Please eat.) (usually shortened to: **Dōzo meshi-agare.** どうぞ 召し上がれ。)

gohan ご飯 rice

ringo りんご apple

pan パン bread

o-sembei おせんべい rice crackers

tamago たまご eggs

o-tōfu お豆腐 bean curd

o-satō お砂糖 sugar

o-shio お塩 salt

yasai 野菜 vegetables

gyūnyū, miruku 牛乳、ミルク milk

o-cha お茶 Japanese tea

(o-)soba (お)そば noodles

buta-niku ぶた肉 pork

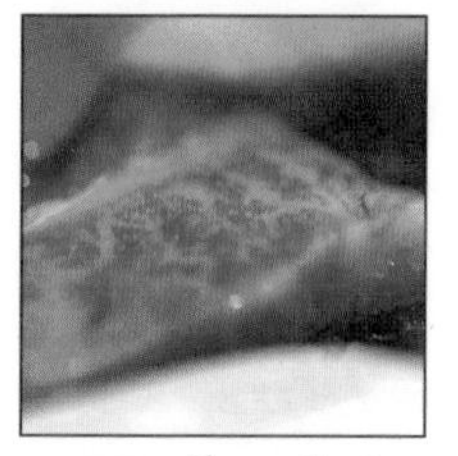
gyū-niku 牛肉 beef

sakana 魚 fish

PHRASES

Dōzo omeshi-agari kudasai. どうぞ お召し上り ください。
(usually shortened to **Dōzo meshi-agare.** どうぞ 召し上がれ。)
Please help yourself. (Please do eat.)

Arigatō-gozaimahss. ありがとうございます。 Thank you.

Itadakimahss. いただきます。 I shall (eat)., Let's eat.

Gohan-wa shiroi dess. ご飯は　白い　です。
Cooked rice is white.

Ringo-wa akai dess. りんごは　赤い　です。
An apple is red.

Pan-wa yawarakai dess. パンは　やわらかい　です。
(The) bread is soft.

O-sembei-wa katai dess. おせんべいは　硬い　です。
The rice crackers are hard.

Tamago-wa marui dess. たまごは　丸い　です。
An egg is round.

O-tōfu-wa shiakui dess. お豆腐は　四角い　です。
The bean curd is square.

O-satō-wa amai dess. お砂糖は　甘い　です。
The sugar is sweet.

O-shio-wa karai dess. お塩は　辛い　です。
The salt is salty.

Gyūnyū-wa tsumetai dess. 牛乳は　冷たい　です。
The milk is cold.

O-cha-wa atsui dess. お茶は　熱い　です。
The tea is hot.

Yasai-wa shinsen dess. 野菜は　新鮮　です。
The vegetables are fresh.

O-soba-wa nagai dess. おそばは　長い　です。
The noodles are long.

Gyuniku-wa oishii dess. 牛肉は　おいしい　です。
(The) beef is tasty.

EXERCISES

Refer to the pictures on the right and fill in the blanks.

1. **O-satō-wa __________ dess.**
   The sugar is sweet.

2. **O-cha-wa __________ dess.**
   The tea is hot.

3. **__________ __________ dess.**
   Cooked rice is white.

4. **__________ karai ________.**
   The salt is salty.

5. **Buta-niku-wa _________ dess.**
   (The) pork is tasty.

6. **Sakana-wa _________ dess.**
   (The) fish is fresh.

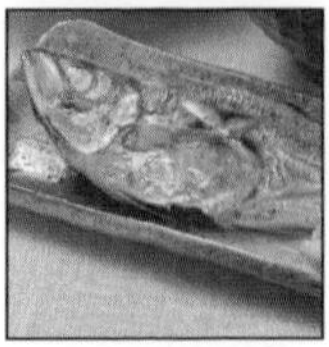

LESSON 13

How is the weather?

VOCABULARY

dō どう how

ii (yoi) いい（よい） good

warui 悪い bad

o-tenki, tenki お天気、天気 weather

ame 雨 rain

kumori 曇り cloudy

yuki 雪 snow

PHRASES

O-tenki-wa dō dess-ka? お天気は どう ですか?
How is the weather?

Ii (yoi) o-tenki dess. いい（よい）お天気 です。
The weather is good.

Warui o-tenki dess. Ame dess. 悪い お天気 です。雨 です。
The weather is bad. It is raining.

Kumori dess. 曇り です。 It is cloudy.

Yuki dess. 雪 です。 It is snowing.

EXERCISES

Refer to the pictures on the right and choose the answer.

O-tenki-wa dō dess-ka?

1. a) **Yuki dess.** It is snowing.
   b) **Ii o-tenki dess.** The weather is good.
   c) **Ame dess.** It is raining.

2. a) **Kumori dess.** It is cloudy.
   b) **Warui o-tenki dess.** The weather is bad.
   c) **Ii o-tenki dess.** The weather is good.

3. a) **Ame dess.** It is raining.
   b) **Kumori dess.** It is cloudy.
   c) **Yuki dess.** It is snowing.

4. a) **Ii o-tenki dess.** The weather is good.
   b) **Warui o-tenki dess.** The weather is bad.
   c) **Yuki dess.** It is snowing.

LESSON 14

Review

VOCABULARY

hon 本 book

kōhii コーヒー coffee

o-mizu お水 water

EXERCISES

1. **Kore-wa nan dess-ka?**
   What is this?
   ___________ ___________ **dess.**

2. **Anata-wa kōhii-ga suki dess-ka?**
   Do you like coffee?
   _________ _________ _________ .

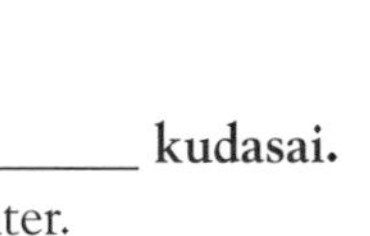

3. **Dōzo watashi-ni ___________ kudasai.**
   Please give me some water.

   Arigatō-gozaimahss.
   Thank you.

4. **Kyō-wa nan nichi dess-ka?** __________ __________ **dess.**
   What day of the month is it today?

5. **Kyō-wa nan yobi dess-ka?** __________ __________ **dess.**
   What day of the week is it today?

6. **Kyō-no o-tenki-wa dō dess-ka?** __________ __________ **dess.**
   How is the weater today?

7. Choose the appropriate response.

Komban-wa. (a)	a. Good evening.
Oyasumi-nasai. ( )	b. Goodbye.
Konnichi-wa. ( )	c. Congratulations.
Sayōnara. ( )	d. Thank you.
Irasshaimase. ( )	e. Welcome. (Please come in.)
Omedetō-gozaimahss. ( )	f. Good day. (Hello. Good afternoon.)
Arigatō-gozaimahss. ( )	g. Good morning.
Gomen-nasai. ( )	h. Good night.
Ohayō-gozaimahss. ( )	i. I am sorry. (Excuse me. Pardon me.)

8. Circle the correct answer.

roku	9	7	4	6	2
ni-jū-san	33	21	15	11	23
go-hyaku	211	510	100	500	300
hachi-jū-hachi	24	36	88	49	18
sen-kyū-hyaku roku-jū-san	185	1226	1963	1684	1953

LESSON 15

Let's go shopping!

VOCABULARY

kaimono 買物 shopping

ikimashō 行きましょう let's go

kore これ this (pronoun, for near objects)

are/sore あれ／それ that (pronoun, for distant objects)

ikura いくら how much

(o-)mise (お)店 shop, store

depāto デパート department store

ni-hyaku en 200円 200 yen

sanman en 30,000円 30,000 yen

goman nana-sen en 57,000円 57,000 yen

yon-sen en 4,000円 4,000 yen

hassen en 8,000円 8,000 yen

hyaku en 100円 100 yen

jū-man en 100,000円 100,000 yen

ni-sen en 2,000円 2,000 yen

sūpā(māketto) スーパー(マーケット) supermarket

momo もも peach

shinju 真珠 pearl

kamera カメラ camera

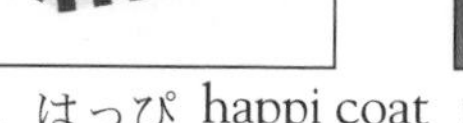

happi はっぴ happi coat

ningyō 人形 doll

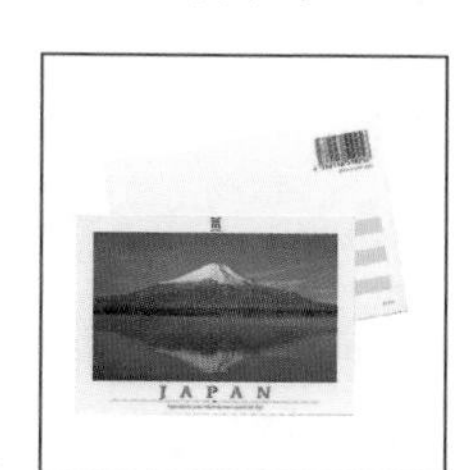

hagaki 葉書 postcard

pasokon パソコン
personal computer/PC

shokki 食器 dinnerware

PHRASES

Kaimono-ni ikimashō! 買物に　行きましょう! Let's go shopping!

X-wa doko-de kaemahss-ka? Xは　どこで　買えますか？
Where can I buy X?

X-wa depāto-de kaemahss. Xは　デパートで　買えます。
You can buy X at department store.

Kore-wa ikura dess-ka? これは　いくら　ですか？
How much is this?

Kore-wa hyaku en dess. これは　100円　です。
This is 100 yen.

Kore-wa yon-sen en dess. これは　4,000円　です。
This is 4,000 yen.

Are(Sore)-wa ikura dess-ka? あれ(それ)は　いくら　ですか？
How much is that (over there)?

Are(Sore)-wa sanman en dess. あれ(それ)は　30,000円　です。
That (it) is 30,000 yen.

X-wa ikura dess-ka? Xは　いくら　ですか? How much is X?

X-wa 8,000 en dess. Xは　8000円　です。 X is 8000 yen.

EXERCISES

Refer to the pictures on the right and fill in the price amount.

1. **Ningyō-wa ikura dess-ka?**
   How much is the doll?

   Ningyō-wa ________________ dess.
   The doll is 8,000 yen.

2. **Hagaki-wa ________________ dess.**
   The postcard is 100 yen.

3. **Pasokon-wa ________________ dess.**
   The PC is 100,000 yen.

4. **Shinju-wa doko-de kaemahss-ka?**
   Where can I buy the pearl?

   Shinju-wa __________ kaemahss.
   You can buy the pearl at department store.

5. **Kamera-wa ikura dess-ka?**
   How much is the camera?

   Camera-wa ________________ dess.
   The camera is 57,000 yen.

6. **Momo-wa doko-de kaemahss-ka?**
   Where can I buy the peach?

   Momo-wa ________________ kaemahss.
   You can buy the peach at supermarket.

LESSON 16

How are you feeling?

VOCABULARY

atama 頭 head

ha 歯 tooth, teeth

o-naka お腹 stomach

byōki 病気 ill, illness

itai 痛い painful, aching

gokigen ごきげん feeling, state of health

kusuri 薬 medicine

isha 医者 doctor

genki 元気
well, fine, healthy

atama-ga itai
頭が 痛い
headache

ha-ga itai
歯が 痛い
toothache

onaka-ga itai
お腹が 痛い
stomach ache

netsu 熱 fever

kaze(-o hiku)
風邪(をひく)
(catch a) cold

PHRASES

Gokigen ikaga dess-ka? ごきげん いかが ですか?
How are you?

Watashi-wa genki dess. 私は 元気 です。 I am well. (I am fine.)

Atama-ga itai dess. 頭が 痛い です。
I have a headache. (My head aches.)

Ha-ga itai dess. 歯が 痛い です。
I have a toothache. (My tooth aches.)

O-naka-ga itai dess. お腹が 痛い です。
I have a stomach ache. (My stomach aches.)

Netsu-ga arimahss. 熱が あります。 I have a fever.

Kaze-o hikimashta. 風邪を ひきました。 I caught a cold.

EXERCISES

1. **Atama-ga ________ dess.**
   I have a headache.

2. **____________ itai dess.**
   I have a stomach ache.

3. **____________ itai dess.**
   I have a toothache.

4. **Kaze-o ____________ .**
   I caught a cold.

5. **____________ arimahss.**
   I have a fever.

LESSON 17

Body Parts

VOCABULARY

atama 頭 head
kami-no-ke, ke 髪の毛、毛 hair
hitai 額 forehead
me 目 eye
hana 鼻 nose
mimi 耳 ear
hoho 頬 cheek
kuchi 口 mouth
ago あご chin
nodo のど throat

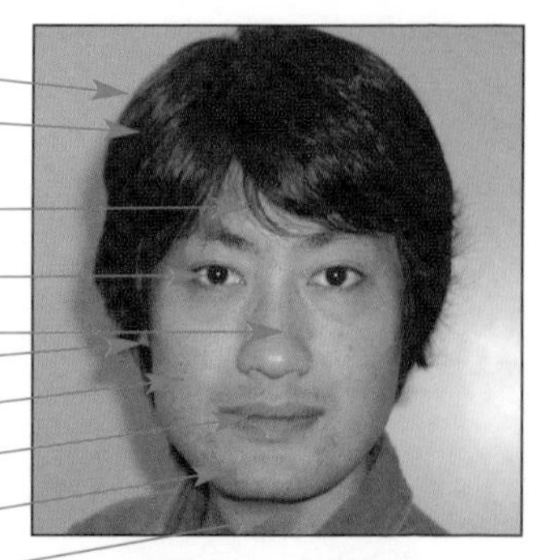

kao 顔 face

te 手 hand
kubi 首 neck
kata 肩 shoulder
ude 腕 arm
mune 胸 chest
hiza ひざ knee
o-naka お腹 stomach
ashi 足 foot, leg
ashi-no-yubi 足の指 toes

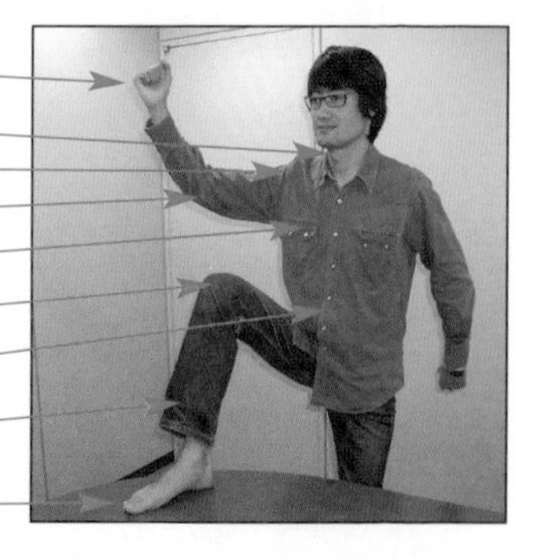

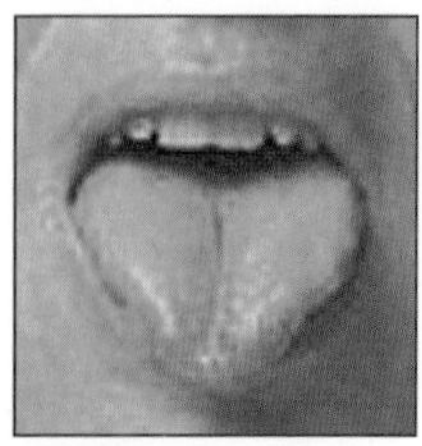

shita 舌 tongue

yubi 指 fingers

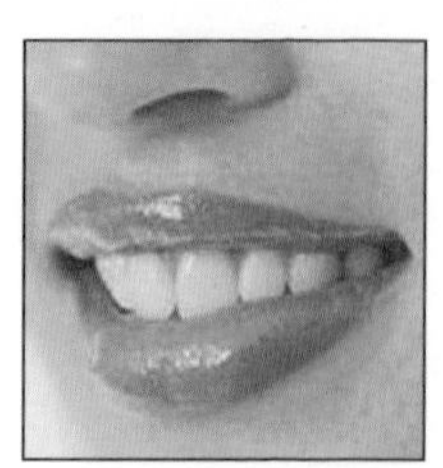

ha 歯 teeth

Clothing

bōshi 帽子 hat
megane めがね eyeglasses
shatsu シャツ shirt
nekutai ネクタイ tie
uwagi 上着 jacket (coat)
beruto ベルト belt
tokei 時計 watch
zubon ズボン pants
kasa 傘 umbrella
kutsu 靴 shoes

EXERCISES

Refer to the pictures on the right and fill in the blanks.

Kore-wa nan dess-ka? What is this?

1. **Kore-wa ________ dess.**
   This is a nose.

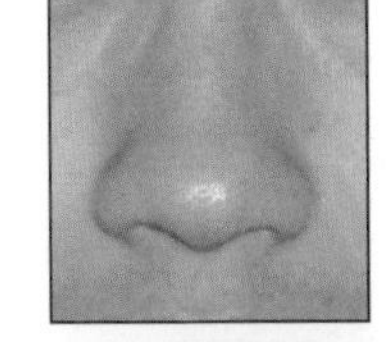

2. **Kore-wa ________ dess.**
   This is an ear.

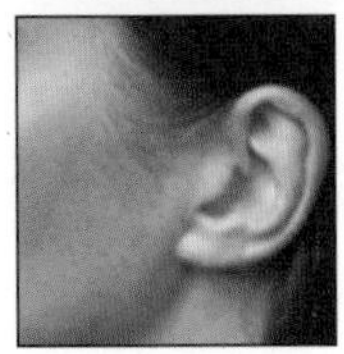

3. **Kore-wa _______ dess.**
These are hands.

4. **Kore-wa _______ dess.**
This is a foot.

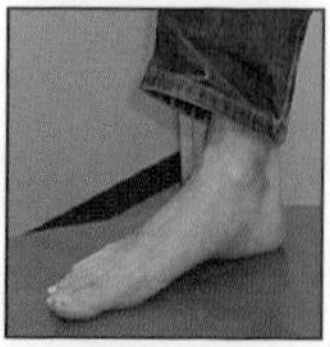

5. **Kore-wa _______ dess.**
These are eyes.

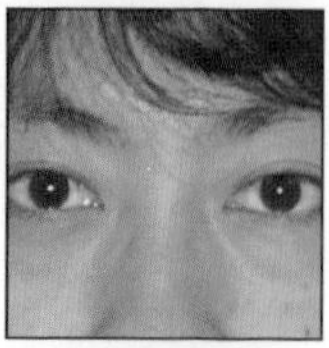

6. **Kore-wa _______ dess.**
This is a hat.

7. **Kore-wa _______ dess.**
This is a tie.

8. **Kore-wa _______ dess.**
This is a shoe.

9. **Kore-wa _______ dess.**
This is a jacket (coat).

LESSON 18

You and I, your and my

VOCABULARY

wata(k)shi-no 私の my

anata-no あなたの your

kaban かばん bag

tomodachi 友達（お友達）
friend (sometimes **o-tomodachi**)

PHRASES

Watashi-wa anata-no tomodachi dess.
私は　あなたの　友達　です。I am your friend.

Anata-wa watashi-no tomodachi dess.
あなたは　私の　友達　です。You are my friend.

Watashi-wa anata-no sensei dess.
私は　あなたの　先生　です。I am your teacher.

Anata-wa watashi-no sensei dess.
あなたは　私の　先生　です。You are my teacher.

Kore-wa anata-no kaban dess-ka?
これは　あなたの　かばん　ですか? Is this your bag?

Kore-wa watashi-no kaban dess.
これは　私の　かばん　です。This is my bag.

Kore-wa watashi-no uwagi dess.
これは　私の　上着　です。This is my jacket.

Kore-wa anata-no raitā dess-ka?
これは　あなたの　ライター　ですか? Is this your lighter?

EXERCISES

1. **Anata-wa __________ sensei dess.**
   You are my teacher.

2. **Anata-wa __________ tomodachi dess.**
   You are my friend.

3. **Watashi-wa __________ sensei dess.**
   I am your teacher.

4. **Kore-wa _________ kaban dess-ka?**
   Is this your bag?

5. **Are-wa _________ jidōsha dess-ka?**
   Is that your car?

6. **Kore-wa _________ hon dess.**
   This is my book.

7. **Watashi-wa __________ tomodachi dess.**
   I am your friend.

8. **Kore-wa _________ _________ dess.**
   This is my jacket.

9. **Are-wa _________ _________ dess-ka?**
   Is that your your lighter?

10. **Are-wa _________ _________ dess-ka?**
    Is that your book?

11. **Kore-wa _________ _________ dess.**
    This is my bag.

12. **Kore-wa _________ hon dess.**
    This is your book.

LESSON 19
This and that

VOCABULARY

hata 旗 flag

doa ドア door

yūmei 有名 famous

utsukushii 美しい beautiful

kawaii かわいい cute, pretty

kono この this (adjective)

ano あの that (adjective, for faraway objects)

sono その that (adjective, for nearby objects)

yōfuku 洋服
dress, clothes

bara バラ rose

deguchi 出口
exit

o-kashi お菓子
cake, candy

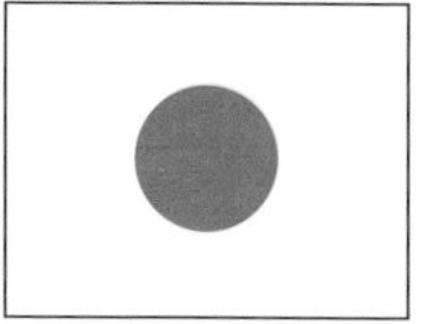
Nihon-no hata
日本の旗 Japanese flag

jisho 辞書
dictionary

PHRASES

Kore-wa yōfuku dess. Kono yōfuku-wa kawaii dess.
これは　洋服　です。 この　洋服は　かわいい　です。
This is a dress. This dress is pretty.

Are-wa bara dess. Ano bara-wa utsukushii dess.
あれは　バラ　です。 あの　バラは　美しい　です。
That is a rose. That rose is beautiful.

Sore-wa hoteru dess. Sono hoteru-wa yūmei dess.
それは　ホテル　です。その　ホテルは　有名　です。
It is the hotel. The hotel is famous.

Kore-wa doa dess. Kono doa-wa deguchi dess.
これは　ドア　です。この　ドアは　出口　です。
This is the door. This door is an exit.

Kore-wa o-kashi dess. Kono o-kashi-wa amai dess.
これは　お菓子　です。この　お菓子は　甘い　です。
This is a candy. This candy is sweet.

Aore-wa hata dess. Aono hata-wa Nihon-no-hata dess.
あれは　旗　です。あの　旗は　日本の旗　です。
That is a flag. That flag is Japanese flag.

Sore-wa hon dess. Sono hon-wa jisho dess.
それは　本　です。その　本は　辞書　です。
That(It) is a book. That book is a dictionary.

EXERCISES

Refer to the pictures on the right and fill in the blanks.

1. **Kore-wa _______________ dess.**
   This is candy.

   Kono o-kashi-wa _______________ dess.
   This candy is sweet.

2. **Kore-wa ______________ dess.**
   This is a flag.

   Kono hata-wa ________________ dess.
   This flag is a Japanese flag.

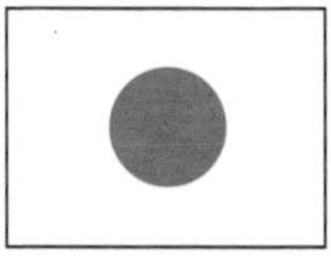

3. **Sore-wa ______________ dess.**
   It is a book.

   Sono hon-wa ____________ dess.
   That book is a dictionary.

4. **Are-wa ______________ dess.**
   That is a rose.

   _______ hana-wa ________ dess.
   That rose is beautiful.

5. **Kore-wa ______________ dess.**
   This is a dress.

   _______ yōfuku-wa ________ dess.
   This dress is pretty.

6. **Kore-wa ______________ dess.**
   This is the door.

   _______ doa-wa ________ dess.
   This door is an exit.

7. **Sore-wa ______________ dess.**
   It is the hotel.

   _______ hoteru-wa _______ dess.
   The hotel is famous.

LESSON 20

Adjectives

VOCABULARY

hane 羽 feather

yōji 楊枝 toothpick

se 背 height (of a person)

adjective form -i –い

omoi 重い heavy

karui 軽い light

nagai 長い long

mijikai 短い short

hayai 速い fast

osoi 遅い slow, late

hikui 低い low, short (in height)

Fujisan 富士山 Mt. Fuji

keshiki 景色 scenery

akai 高い tall, high

ōkii 大きい large

chiisa 小さい small

atarashii 新しい new

furui 古い old

marui 丸い round

shikakui 四角い square

utsukushii 美しい beautiful

ishi 石 stone

kami 紙 paper

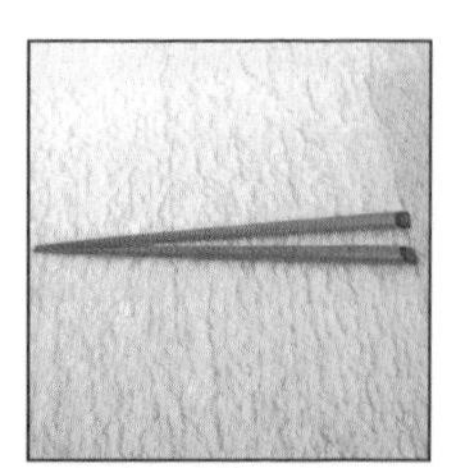

hashi 箸 chopsticks

jettoki ジェット機 jet plane

densha 電車 train

kodomo 子供 child

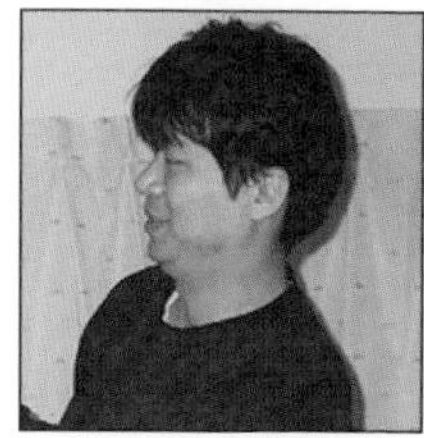

otona 大人 adult

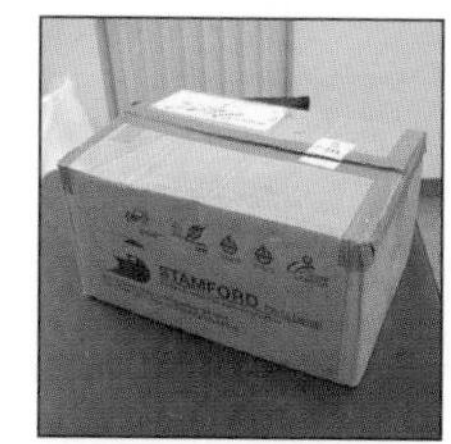

hako 箱 box

bōru ボール ball

靴下 socks

takushii タクシー taxi

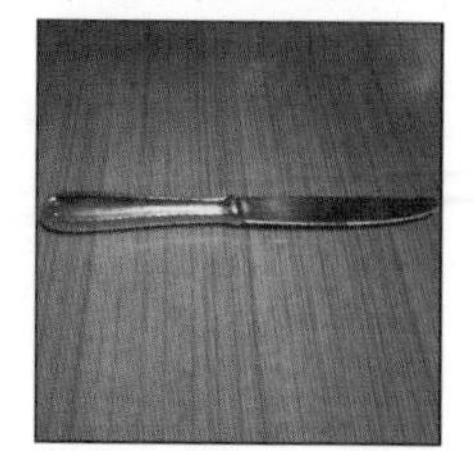

naifu ナイフ knife

PHRASES

Kono ishi-wa omoi dess. この 石は 重い です。
This stone is (these stones are) heavy.

Kami-wa karui dess. 紙は 軽い です。
A (sheet of) paper is light.

Hashi-wa nagai dess. 箸は 長い です。
The chopsticks are long.

Yōji-wa mijikai dess. 楊枝は 短い です。
This toothpick is short.

Jettoki-wa hayai dess. ジェット機は　速い　です。
A jet plane is fast.

Densha-wa osoi dess. 電車は　遅い　です。 A train is slow.

Kodomo-no se-wa hikui dess. 子供の　背は　低い　です。
A child's height is low. (A child is short.)

Otona-no se-wa takai dess. 大人の　背は　高い　です。
An adult's height is tall.

Kono hako-wa ōkii dess. この　箱は　大きい　です。
This box is large.

Kono bōru-wa chiisai dess. この　ボールは　小さい　です。
This ball is small.

Watashi-no kutsu-wa atarashii dess.
私の　靴は　新しい　です。 My shoes are new.

Anata-no kutsushita-wa furui dess.
あなたの　靴下は　古い　です。 Your socks are old.

EXERCISES

Fill in the blanks.

1. **Kami-wa omoi dess-ka?**
   Is a (sheet of) paper heavy?

   Iie, kami-wa __________ dess.
   No, a paper is light.

2. **Kono hako-wa chiisai dess-ka?**
   Is this box small?

   Iie, kono hako-wa __________ dess.
   No, this box is big.

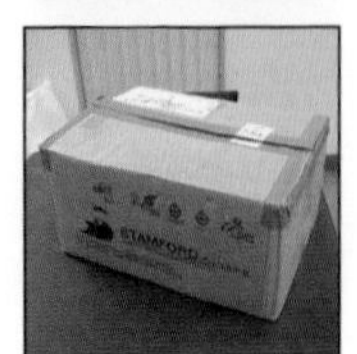

3. **Jettoki-wa ________ dess-ka?**
   Is a jet plane fast?

   Hai, jettoki-wa __________ dess.
   Yes, a jet plane is fast.

4. **Kono bōru-wa ōkii dess-ka?**
   Is this ball big?

   Iie, kono bōru-wa __________ dess.
   No, this ball is small.

5. **Anata-no kutsu-wa furui dess-ka?**
   Are your shoes old?

   Iie, __________ kutsu-wa __________ dess.
   No, my shoes are new.

6. **Takushii-wa ________ dess-ka?**
   Is a taxi fast?

   Iie, takushii-wa __________ dess.
   A taxi is slow.

Refer to the pictures on the right and choose the correct adjectives:

1. **Hashi-wa** { **omoi** heavy / **nagai** long / **mijikai** short } **dess.**
   The copstickes are long.

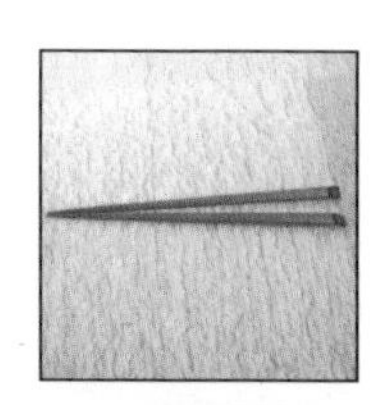

2. **Yōji-wa** { **nagai** long / **okii** big / **mijikai** short } **dess.**
   The toothpick is short.

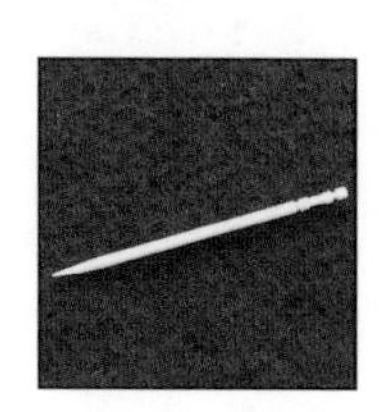

3. **Kono kutsu-wa** { **furui** old / **atarashii** new / **utsukushii** beautiful } **dess.**

This shoe is new.

4. **Kono bōru-wa** { **mijikai** short / **marui** round / **shikakui** square } **dess.**

This ball is new.

5. **Kono hako-wa** { **nagai** long / **shikakui** square / **marui** round } **dess.**

This box is square.

6. **Densha-wa** { **hayai** fast / **karui** light / **osoi** slow } **dess.**

The train is slow.

Fill in the blanks:

7. **Fujisan-wa ________ yama dess.**
   Mt. Fuji is a high mountain.

8. **Watashi-wa ________ yōfuku-o kaimashta.**
   I bought a new dress (clothes).

9. **Watashi-wa ________ keshiki-ga suki dess.**
   I love the beautiful scenery.

10. **Kono bōru-wa ________ dess.**
    This ball is round.

11. **Kono nimotsu-wa ________ dess.**
    This luggage is heavy.

LESSON 21

Adverbs

VOCABULARY

adverb form – ku – く

hayaku 速く／早く fast, early, quickly

osoku 遅く slowly, late

hikuku 低く low

takaku 高く high

omoku 重く heavily

karuku 軽く lightly

nagaku 長く long

mijikaku 短く short

utsukushiku 美しく beautifully

yoku 良く well

akaku 赤く red

tsumetaku 冷たく cold

kimashta 来ました came

ikimahss 行きます go, goes

tobimahss 飛びます fly, flies

tobimashta 飛びました flew

narimahss なります become, becomes

narimashta なりました became (got turned into, etc.)

imahss います am, is, are, have been, has been

kiremahss 切れます cut, cuts

kirimashta 切りました cut (past tense)

sakimahss 咲きます bloom, blooms

benkyō 勉強 a study (noun)

shimahss します do, does

Nihongo 日本語 Japanese

dekimahss できます can

NOTE: The formation and use of adverbs in Japanese is somewhat different from that in English. The chief difference to be noted here is that **narimahss** (become, becomes) and **narimashta** (became) are used with an adverb in Japanese rather than with an adjective as in English.

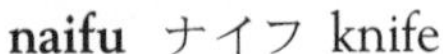

naifu ナイフ knife **tori** 鳥 birds

PHRASES

Watashi-wa hayaku ikimahss. 私は　早く　行きます。
I shall go quickly (early).

Watashi-wa osoku kimashta. 私は　遅く　来ました。
I came late.

Ano tori-wa hiku-ku tobimahss. あの　鳥は　低く　飛びます。
That bird is flying low.

Jettoki-wa takaku tobimashta. ジェット機は　高く　飛びました。
The jet plane flew high.

Nimotsu-ga omoku narimashta. 荷物が　重く　なりました。
The luggage is getting (becoming) heavy.

Nimotsu-ga karuku narimashta. 荷物が　軽く　なりました。
The luggage became light.

Watashi-wa nagaku Nihon-ni imahss.
私は　長く　日本に　います。
I have been in Japan for a long time.

Watashi-wa kami-no-ke-o mijikaku kirimashta.
私は　髪の毛を　短く　切りました。
I cut my hair short. (I have my hair cut short.)

Hana-wa utsukushiku sakimahss. 花は　美しく　咲きます。
The flowers are blooming beautifully.

Anata-wa Nihongo-ga yoku dekimahss.
あなたは　日本語が　良く　できます。
You can speak Japanese well.

Kono kaifu-wa yoku kiremahss.
この　ナイフは　良く　切れます。This knife cuts well.

Ringo-wa akaku narimahss. りんごは　赤く　なります。
The apples are turning (becoming) red.

EXERCISES

Fill in the blanks:

1. **Watashi-ni kippu-o ________ kudasai.**
   Please give me a ticket quickly.

2. **Gakusei-wa ________ benkyō shimahss.**
   The student studies well.

3. **Hikōki-wa ________ tobimahss.**
   The airplane flies high.

4. **Watashi-wa ________ kimashta.**
   I came late.

5. **O-cha-ga ________ narimashta.**
   The tea became cold.

6. **Ringo-wa ________ narimahss.**
   The apples are turning (becoming) red.

7. **Watashi-wa kami-no-ke-o ________ kirimashta.**
   I cut my hair short. (I have my hair cut short.)

8. **Hana-wa ________ sakimahss.**
   The flowers are blooming beautifully.

9. **Nimotsu-ga ________ narimashta.**
   The luggage became light.

10. **Watashi-wa ________ Nihon-ni imahss.**
    I have been in Japan for a long time.

LESSON 22

Many and much, little and few

VOCABULARY

takusan たくさん a lot of, many, much

sukoshi 少し a few, a little

ikutsu いくつ how many

sukoshi-mo 少しも none (with negative verb)

mada まだ still, yet

arimahss あります is, are, there is, there are

arimasen ありません is not, are not,

imahss います is, are (of living creatures)

PHRASES

Hon-wa takusan arimahss-ka? 本は たくさん ありますか?
Are there a lot of books? (Are there many books?)

Hai, takusan arimahss. はい、たくさん あります。
Yes, there are a lot. (Yes, there are.)

Iie, takusan arimasen. いいえ、たくさん ありません。
No, there aren't many.

Sukoshi arimahss. 少し あります。 There are a few.

Sukoshi-mo arimasen. 少しも ありません。
There aren't any. (There are none.)

X-wa mada takusan arimahss-ka?
X は まだ たくさん ありますか? Are there a lot of X?

Ikutsu arimahss-ka? いくつ ありますか? How many?

EXERCISES

Refer to the pictures on the right and fill in the blanks.

1. **Gohan-wa takusan arimahss-ka?**
   Are there much cooked rice?

   Hai, __________ arimahss.
   Yes, there are much.

2. **Tori-wa takusan imahss-ka?**
   Are there many birds?

   __________ , __________ imahss.
   Yes, there are many.

3. **Anata-wa hon-o takusan motte-imahss-ka?**
   Do you have many books?

   Hai, __________ motte-imahss.
   Yes, I have many.

4. **Isu-wa takusan arimahss-ka?**
   There are a lot of chairs?

   Iie, __________ arimasen.
   No, there aren't many.

5. **Ikutsu arimahss-ka? Hitotsu __________.**
   How many. There is one.

6. **Ringo-wa takusan arimahss-ka?**
   There are a lot of apples?

   Iie, __________ arimasen.
   No, there aren't many.

   __________ arimahss.
   There is one.

LESSON 23
Where is it?

VOCABULARY

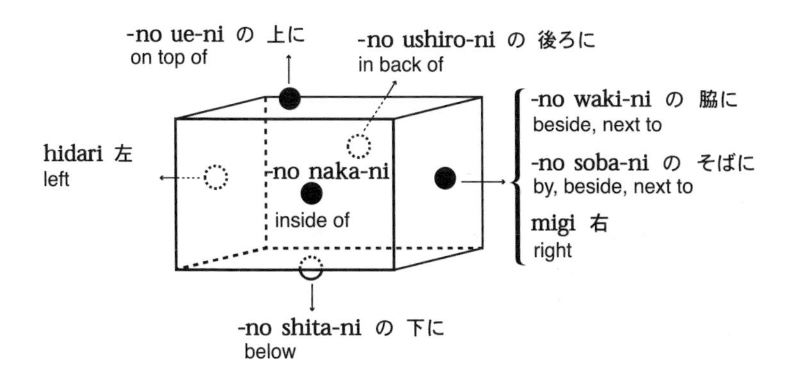

doko-ni どこ where (with suffix indicating location "at")

-no naka-ni の 中に inside of

-no ue-ni の 上に on top of

-no shita-ni の 下に below

-no ushiro-ni の 後ろに in back of

-no soba-ni の そばに beside, next to

-no waki-ni の 脇に beside, next to

hidari 左 left

migi 右 right

hidari-gawa 左側 left side

migi-gawa 右側 right side

hidari-ni 左に at the left, to the left of

migi-ni 右に at the right, to the right of

pen ペン pen

megane めがね eyeglasses

kumo 雲 cloud

yūbinposto 郵便ポスト mailbox

hikidashi-no naka-ni
引き出しの 中に
in the drawer

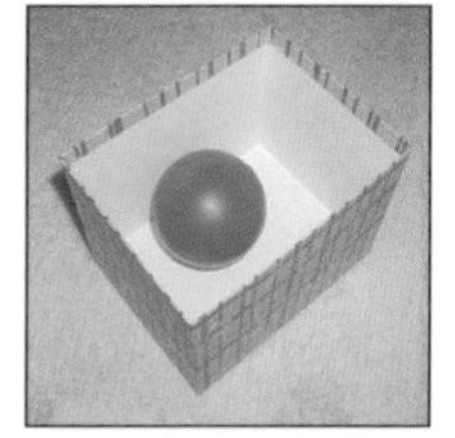

hako-no naka-ni
箱の 中に
in the box

tsukue-no ue-ni
机の 上に
on the desk

kaisha 会社 office

ginkō 銀行 bank

suitchi スイッチ
switch

honya 本屋
bookstore

tsukue 机 desk

hikidashi 引き出し
drawer

sora-no ue-ni
空の 上に
in the sky

michi 道
street, road

denki 電気
light (lamp)

PHRASES

Doko-ni arimahss-ka? どこに　ありますか? Where is it?

Pen-wa doko-ni arimahss-ka? ペンは　どこに　ありあますか?
Where is the pen?

Pen-wa tsukue-no ue-ni arimahss.
ペンは　机の　上に　あります。The pen is on the desk.

Megane-wa doko-ni arimahss-ka?
めがねは　どこに　ありますか? Where are the eyeglasses?

Megane-wa hikidashi-no naka-ni arimahss.
めがねは　引き出しの　中に　あります。
The eyeglasses are in the drawer.

Denki-no suitchi-wa doko-ni arimahss-ka?
電気の　スイッチは　どこに　ありますか?
Where is the electric switch?

Sore-wa doa-no waki-ni arimahss.
それは　ドアの　脇に　あります。It is beside the door.

Kumo-wa doko-ni arimahss-ka? 雲は　どこに　ありますか?
Where is the cloud?

Kumo-wa sora-no ue-ni arimahss. 雲は　空の　上に　あります。
The cloud is in the sky.

Ginkō-wa doko-ni arimahss-ka? 銀行は　どこに　ありますか?
Where is the bank?

Ginkō-wa kono michi-no hidari-gawa-ni arimahss.
銀行は　この　道の　左側に　あります。
The bank is on the left side of this street.

Kaisha-wa doko dess-ka? 会社は　どこ　ですか?
Where is your office?

Kaisha-wa hidari-ni arimahss. 会社は　左に　あります。
My office is at (to) the left.

EXERCISES

Refer to the pictures and fill in the blanks.

1. **Bōru-wa doko-ni arimahss-ka?**
   Where is the ball?

   Bōru-wa ________ ________ arimahss.
   The ball is in the box.

2. **Megane-wa doko-ni arimahss-ka?**
   Where are the eyeglasses?

   Megane-wa __________ __________ arimahss.
   The eyeglasses are on the desk.

3. **Hon-ya-wa doko dess-ka?**
   Where are the bookstore?

   Hon-ya-wa kono michi-no __________ arimahss.
   The bookstore is on the left side of this street.

4. **Denki-no suitchi-wa doko-ni arimahss-ka?**
   Where is the electric switch?

   Sore-wa ________-ni arimahss.
   It is on the left side.

5. **Kaisha-wa doko-ni arimahss-ka?**
   Where is the office?

   Kaisha-wa __________-ni arimahss.
   The office is on the right side.

6. **Yūbin posuto-wa doko dess-ka?**
   Where is the mailbox?

   Yūbin posuto-wa _________-ni arimahss.
   The mailbox is at (to) the left.

LESSON 24

Let's make a phone call!

VOCABULARY

denwa 電話 telephone

kakemashō かけましょう (telephone) let's call

moshi, moshi もし、もし hello (on the telephone)

san さん Miss, Mr., Mrs. (never with one's own name)

-mo も too, also

hanasu-koto 話すこと to speak, speaking (noun)

jōzu 上手 well

... ne ...ね ... don't you? ... can't you? ... isn't it? ... aren't you? etc.

dewa では then, well then

Sayōnara さようなら Good bye

PHRASES

John: **Moshi, moshi. Keiko-san dess-ka?**
もし、もし、恵子さん ですか? Hello. Is this Keiko?

Keiko: **Hai, sō dess.** はい、そう です。 Yes, it is.

John: **Watashi-wa John dess. Gokigen ikaga dess-ka?**
私は ジョン です。ごきげん いかが ですか?
This is John. How are you?

Keiko: **Watashi-wa genki dess. Anata-wa ikaga dess-ka?**
私は 元気です。あなたは いかが ですか?
I'm fine. How are you?

John: **Watashi-mo genki dess. Anata-wa Eigo-o hanasukoto-ga dekimahss-ka?** 私も 元気 です。あなたは 英語を 話すことが できますか?
I'm fine too. Can you speak English?

Keiko: **Hai, sukoshi dekimahss. Anata-wa Nihongo-ga jōzu dess ne.** • はい、少し　できます。あなたは　日本語が　上手ですね。
Yes, I can—a little. You can speak Japanese well, can't you?

John: **Arigatō-gozaimahss. Dewa, sayōnara.**
ありがとうございます。では、さようなら。
Thank you. Well then, goodbye.

Hanako: **Sayōnara.** さようなら。 Goodbye.

EXERCISES

Answer the questions.

1. **__________ Keiko-san dess-ka?**
Hello. Is this Keiko?

Hai, sō dess.
Yes, it is.

2. **Watashi-wa __________ dess. __________ ikaga dess-ka?**
This is John. How are you?

3. **Watashi-wa __________ dess. Anata-wa ikaga dess-ka?**
I'm fine. How are you?

4. **Watashi-mo __________ dess.**
I'm fine too.

5. **Dewa, __________ .**
Well then, goodbye.

Sayōnara.
Goodbye.

LESSON 25

A Japanese game and a song

VOCABULARY

haru 春 spring

tori 鳥 bird, birds

naku 鳴く sing, sings

saku 咲く bloom, blooms

kita きた has come, came

no 野 fields

sato 里 village

yama 山 mountains

-de で (suffix indicationg that an action is taking place at the location named)

gū グー ... stone **choki** チョキ ... scissors **pā** パー ... paper

Jan-ken-pon is a very popular game among Japanese children as well as adults. The Japanese people play this game to decide the winner and the loser in everyday activities, just as the Americans flip a coin into the air to decide the same thing.

In this game, three hand signs are used: **gū**, symbolizing stone; **choki**, symbolizing scissors; and **pā**, symbolizing paper. The palm of the hand represents a sheet of paper and is called **pā**. The closed fist represents stone and is called **gū**. Two fingers—the index finger and the middle finger—represent a pair of scissors, called **choki**. Each player makes whichever of these gestures he chooses, and the winner is decided as follows: Paper wraps stone, so paper wins over stone. Stone is too hard for scissors to cut, so stone wins over scissors. Scissors cut paper, so scissors win over paper.

As you play this game, you may sing the following well-known Japanese children's song (ask one of your Japanese friends to teach you the melody):

Haru-ga Kita
春が　きた

1. **Ha-ru-ga ki-ta, ha-ru-ga ki-ta. Doko-ni-ki-ta? Ya-ma-ni ki-ta, sa-to-ni ki-ta, no-ni-mo ki-ta.**
   春が　きた、春が　きた。どこにきた。山に　きた、里に　きた、野にも　きた。

2. **To-ri-ga na-ku, to-ri-ga na-ku. Do-ko-de-na-ku? Ya-ma-de na-ku, sa-to-de na-ku, no-de-mo na-ku.**
   鳥が　鳴く、鳥が　鳴く。どこで鳴く。山で　鳴く、里で　鳴く　野でも　鳴く。

3. **Ha-na-ga sa-ku, ha-na-ga sa-ku. Do-ko-ni-sa-ku? Ya-ma-ni sa-ku, sa-to-ni sa-ku, no-ni-mo sa-ku.**
   花が　咲く、花が　咲く。どこに咲く。山に　咲く。里に　咲く。野にも　咲く。

Vocabulary List

Japanese – English

ago あご chin
aisatsu あいさつ greetings
akai 赤い red (adjective)
akaku 赤く red (adverbial form)
aki 秋 autumn
amai 甘い sweet
ame 雨 rain
Amerika-jin アメリカ人 an American, American people
anata あなた you
anata-ni あなたに to you
anata-no あなたの your
anata-wa あなたは you (nominative)
ano あの that (adjective, for distant objects)
are あれ that (pronoun, for distant objects)
arigatō. ありがとう Thank you. (less formal)
arigatō-gozaimahss. ありがとうございます Thank you. (more formal)
arimasen ありません is not, are not, there is not, there are not
arimahss あります is, are, there is, there are
asa 朝 morning
ashi 足 leg, foot, legs, feet
ashi-no-yubi 足の指 toe, toes
ashita 明日 tomorrow
asu 明日 tomorrow
atama 頭 head
atarashii 新しい new
atatakai 暖かい/温かい warm
atsui 暑い/熱い hot
ban 晩 evening
bara バラ rose
basutei バス停 bus stop
beruto ベルト belt
benkyō 勉強 study (noun)
bijinesu-man ビジネスマン businessman
bōru ボール ball
bōshi 帽子 hat
bubun 部分 part
buta-niku ぶた肉 pork
cha (o-cha) 茶(お茶) tea
chiisai 小さい small, little
chikatetsu no eki 地下鉄の駅 subway station
Chūgoku-jin 中国人 a Chinese, Chinese people
de-wa arimasen では ありません am/is/are not
deguchi 出口 exit
dekimasen できません be unable, cannot
dekimahss できます be able, can
denki 電気 electricity, electric light, electric
densha 電車 train
denwa 電話 telephone
depāto デパート department sotre
deshita でした was, were
desu (des) です am, is, are
dewa では then, well then
dō どう how
doa ドア door
Doitsu-jin ドイツ人 a German, German people
doko どこ where
dōmo どうも very much
dore どれ which
Do-yōbi 土曜日 Saturday
dōzo どうぞ please
Eigo 英語 English language
eki 駅 station

empitsu えんぴつ pencil
en 円 yen
fōku フォーク fork
Fujisan 富士山 Mt. Fuji
fukushi 副詞 adverb
fun (pun) 分 minute
Furansu-jin フランス人 a French, French people
furui 古い old
futari 二人 two persons
futatsu 二つ two
futsuka 二日 second (day of the month)
fuyu 冬 winter
-ga が (nominative postposition)
gakusei 学生 student
genki 元気 healthy, fine, well
geta 下駄 wooden clogs
Getsu-yōbi 月曜日 Monday
ginkō 銀行 bank
go 五 five
gochisō-sama. ごちそうさま (everyday expression said after eating)
Go-gatsu 五月 May
gogo 午後 afternoon, P.M.
gohan ご飯 cooked rice
gokigen ごきげん feeling, state of health
gomen-nasai. ごめんなさい I am sorry, excuse me, pardon me
gorufu ゴルフ golf
gozen 午前 morning, A.M.
gyūniku 牛肉 beef
gyūnyū 牛乳 milk
ha 歯 tooth, teeth
hachi 八 eight
Hachi-gatsu 八月 August
hagaki 葉書 postcard
hai はい yes
haizara 灰皿 ashtray
hako 箱 box
han 半 half
hana 花 flower
hana 鼻 nose
hanasu-koto 話すこと to speak, speaking (noun)
happi はっぴ happi coat
haru 春 spring
hashi (o-hashi) 箸（お箸） chopsticks
hata 旗 flag
hatsuka 二十日 twentieth (day of the month)
hayai 速い／早い fast, quick, early (adjective)
hayaku 速く／早く fast, quickly, early (adverb)
heya 部屋 room
hidari 左 left (direction)
hidari-gawa 左側 left side
hikidashi 引き出し drawer
hikōki 飛行機 airplane
hikui 低い low, short (in height)
hikuku 低く low (adverbial form)
hiru 昼 afternoon, noon, p.m.
hitai 額 forehead
hitori 一人 one person
hitotsu 一つ one
hiza 膝 knee
hoho 頬 cheek
hon 本 book
hon-ya 本屋 bookshop
hoteru ホテル hotel
hyaku 百 hundred
hyōgen 表現 expression (in speech)
ichi 一 one
ichi 位置 position
Ichi-gatsu 一月 January
Igirisu-jin イギリス人 a British, British people
ii (yoi) いい（良い） good, fine
iie いいえ no (interjection)
ikaga いかが how?
ikimahss (yukimahss) 行きます go, goes
ikura いくら how much
ikutsu いくつ how many
imahss います is, are, am
imasen いません is not, are not, am not
inu 犬 dog

irasshaimase. いらっしゃいませ Welcome. Please come in.
isha 医者 doctor
ishi 石 stone, rock
isu 椅子 chair
itadakimahss いただきます (everyday expression, said before eating) I shall (eat). Let's eat.
itai 痛い painful
itsuka 五日 fifth (day of the month)
itsutsu 五つ five
Jan-ken-pon ジャンケンポン (the Japanese game of "scissors, paper and stone")
jettoki ジェット機 jet plane
-ji 時 o'clock, time
jidōsha 自動車 car
jisho 辞書 dictionary
jōzu 上手 very well, be skillful, be good at
jū 十 ten
Jū-gatsu 十月 October
Jū-ichi-gatsu 十一月 November
Jū-ni-gatsu 十二月 December
jūsho 住所 address
-ka か (The sentence that ends with –ka is an interrogative sentence.)
kaban かばん suitcase, brief case
kaimono 買物 shopping
kaisha 会社 office
kakemahss (denwa-o) call （電話を）かけます
kakimahss 書きます write, writes
kaku-koto 書くこと to write, writing (noun)
kamera カメラ camera
kami 紙 paper
kami-no-ke 髪の毛 hair
kao 顔 face
karada 体 body
karai 辛い salty, peppery, spicy
karui 軽い light (adjective)
karuku 軽く lightly (adverb)
kasa 傘 umbrella
kashi (o-kashi) 菓子（お菓子） cake
kata 肩 shoulder
katai 硬い hard, crisp
kawaii かわいい cute, lovely, pretty
Ka-yōbi 火曜日 Tuesday
kaze 風邪 cold
kazu 数 number
ke 毛 hair
keitai denwa 携帯電話 cell phone
keiyōshi 形容詞 adjective
keshiki 景色 scenery
kikō 気候 climate
kimahss 来ます come, comes
kinō 昨日 yesterday
Kinyōbi 金曜日 Friday
kippu 切符 ticket
kirai 嫌い dislike
kiremahss 切れます cut
kirimashta 切りました cut (past tense)
kisetsu 季節 season
kita 来た came, has come
kodomo 子供 child, children
kōhii コーヒー coffee
koko, koko-ni ここ、ここに here
kokonoka 九日 ninth (day of the month)
kokonotsu 九つ nine
komban-wa こんばんは good evening
kongetsu 今月 this month
konnichi-wa こんにちは good day, Hello, Good afternoon
kono この this (adjective)
konshū 今週 this week
kore これ this (pronoun)
kore-wa これは this (pronoun, nominative)
kotae 答え answer
ku 九 nine
kubi 首 neck
kuchi 口 mouth
kudamono くだもの fruit
… kudasai …ください (please) give me
Kugatsu 九月 September
kūkō 空港 airport

kumori 曇り cloudy
kutsu 靴 shoes
kutsushita 靴下 stockings, socks
kyō 今日 today
kyū 九 nine
kyūjitsu 休日 holiday
mada まだ still, yet
mae 前 before, to (in telling time)
man 万 ten thousand
marui 丸い round
me 目 eye, eyes
megane めがね eyeglasses
meshiagare 召し上がれ please help yourself.
michi 道 street, road
migi 右 right (direction)
mijikai 短い short (adjective)
mijikaku 短く short (adverb)
mikka 三日 third (day of the month)
mimi 耳 ear, ears
miruku ミルク milk
mise (o-mise) 店(お店) shop, store
mittsu 三つ three
mizu (o-mizu) 水(お水) water
-mo も too, also
Moku-yōbi 木曜日 Thursday
momo もも peach
moshi, moshi もし、もし hello (on the telephone)
motte-imasen 持っていません have not, has not
motte-imahss 持っています have, has
muika 六日 sixth (day of the month)
mune 胸 chest
muttsu 六つ six
nagai 長い long (adjective)
nagaku 長く long (adverb)
naka 中 inside (noun)
naifu ナイフ knife
naku 鳴く cry, sing (birds)
namae 名前 name
nan-ji 何時 what time?
nan, nani 何 what?
nanoka 七日 seventh (day of the month)
nana, nanatsu 七、七つ seven
napukin ナプキン napkin
narimashta なりました became, grew
narimahss なります become, becomes, grow, grows
natsu 夏 summer
… , ne ね … , isn't it? … , aren't you? … , don't you? etc
nekutai ネクタイ tie
netsu 熱 fever
ni 二 two
-ni に to, at, in, for
nichi 日 day (date)
nichijō 日常 daily, everyday
Nichi-yōbi 日曜日 Sunday
Ni-gatsu 二月 February
Nihon 日本 Japan
Nihongo 日本語 Japanese language
Nihon-jin 日本人 a Japanese, Japanese people
Nihon ryōri 日本料理 Japanese dishes (cooking)
niku 肉 meat
nimotsu 荷物 luggage, package
-nin 人 -people (counting people)
ningyō 人形 doll
no 野 field
-no の of, 's (possessive; postposition for possessive case)
nodo のど throat
-no naka-ni の 中に in, inside
-no shita-ni の 下に under
-no soba-ni の そばに by, beside, next to
-no ue-ni の 上に on, to top of, over
-no ushiro-ni の 後ろに behind
-no waki-ni の 脇に by, beside, next to
-o を (postposition for objective case)
o 尾 tail
o- お (honorific prefix often added to a noun for politeness)
o-cha お茶 tea

Ohayō-gozaimahss おはようございます Good morning
o-hashi お箸 chopsticks
oishii おいしい tasty, delicious
o-kashi お菓子 cake, candy
ōkii 大きい big, large
omedetō-gozaimahss おめでとうございます congratulation
omeshiagari kudasai お召し上がりください please help yourself
o-mise お店 shop, store
o-mizu お水 water
omoi 重い heavy
omoku 重く heavily
o-naka お腹 stomach
ongaku 音楽 music
o-satō お砂糖 sugar
o-sembei おせんべい Japanese rice crackers
o-shio お塩 salt
osoi 遅い slow, late
osoku 遅く slowly, late (adverb)
o-tenki お天気 weather
o-tōfu お豆腐 bean curd
otona 大人 adult, grown-up
oyasumi-nasai おやすみなさい Good night
pasokon パソコン personal computer
pen ペン pen
piano ピアノ piano
pun (fun) 分 minute
raigetsu 来月 next month
raishū 来週 next week
raitā ライター lighter
resutoran レストラン restaurant
ringo りんご apple
roku 六 six
Roku-gatsu 六月 June
ryōri 料理 food, cooking
sakana 魚 fish
sakimahss 咲きます blooms, bloom
sake 酒 sake
saku 咲く blooms, bloom
samui 寒い cold
san 三 three
-san さん Mr., Mrs., Miss
San-gatsu 三月 March
sashimi 刺身 sashimi
sato 里 village
satō (o-satō) 砂糖（お砂糖） sugar
sayōnara. さようなら Goodbye
se 背 height (of a person)
sembei (o-sembei) せんべい（おせんべい） Japanese rice crackers
sen 千 thousand
sengetsu 先月 last month
sensei 先生 teacher
senshū 先週 last week
shatsu シャツ shirt
shi 四 four
shichi 七 seven
Shichi-gatsu 七月 July
Shi-gatsu 四月 April
shikakui 四角い square
shimahss します do, does
shimbun 新聞 newspaper
shinju 真珠 pearl, pearls
shinkansen 新幹線 bullet train
shinsen 新鮮 fresh
shio (o-shio) 塩（お塩） salt
shiroi 白い white
shita 舌 tongue
shita 下 bottom, lower part, foot (of hill)
shokki 食器 dinnerware
shū 週 week
sō そう so, exactly!
soba そば noodles
soko, soko-ni そこ、そこに there
sono その that (adjective, for non-distant objects)
sora 空 sky
sore それ that (pronoun, for non-distant objects)
sore-wa それは that (pronoun, nominative, for non-distant objects)
sugi 過ぎ after, past (in telling time)
suitchi スイッチ switch
suiyōbi 水曜日 Wednesday
suki 好き like
sukoshi 少し a little, a few

sukoshi-mo 少しも none
sumimasen (suimasen) すみません（すいません） sorry, thank you
sūpāmāketto スーパーマーケット supermarket
supūn スプーン spoon
sushi すし sushi
suzushii 涼しい cool
tabako たばこ cigarette
tabemono 食べ物 food
taberu-koto 食べること to eat, eating (noun)
tadashii 正しい right, correct
takai 高い high, tall
takaku 高く high (adverb)
takusan たくさん a lot of, many, much
takushii タクシー taxi
tamago たまご egg
tango 単語 vocabulary
tate 縦 vertical
te 手 hand
tenki (o-tenki) 天気（お天気） weather
tō 十 ten
tobimahss 飛びます fly, flies (verb)
tōfu (o-tofu) 豆腐（お豆腐） bean curd
tōka 十日 tenth (day of the month)
tokei 時計 watch, clock
Tōkyō 東京 capital city of Japan
tomodachi (o-tomodachi) 友達（お友達） friend
tori 鳥 bird
tsuitachi 一日 first (day of the month)
tsuki 月 month
tsukue 机 desk
tsumetai 冷たい cool, cold
tsumetaku 冷たく cool, cold
uchi 家 house, home
ude 腕 arm
ue 上 top, upper part
ushiro 後ろ back, rear (noun)
utsukushii 美しい beautiful
utsukushiku 美しく beautifully
uwagi 上着 jacket, coat
-wa は (nominative postposition)
waki 脇 side
warui 悪い bad
watashi (watakshi) 私 I
watashi-ni (watakshi-ni) 私に to me
watashi-no (watakshi-no) 私の my
watashi-wa (watakshi-wa) 私は I
-ya 屋 store, shop
yama 山 mountain
yasai 野菜 vegetable, vegetables
yattsu 八つ eight
yawarakai 柔らかい soft
yōbi 曜日 days of the week
yōka 八日 eighth (days of the month)
yokka 四日 yokka (days of the month)
yo, yon 四 four
yōbi 曜日 day of the week
yōfuku 洋服 clothes, dress (Western style)
yoi (ii) 良い good, fine
yōji 楊枝 toothpick
yoko 横 horizontal
yoku 良く well
yomu-koto 読むこと to read, reading (noun)
yottsu 四つ four
yubi 指 finger
yūgata 夕方 evening
yuki 雪 snow
yukimahss (ikimahss) 行きます go, goes
yuku-koto (iku-koto) 行くこと to go, going (noun)
yūmei 有名 famous
zōri 草履 sandals
zubon ズボン pants

English – Japanese

a few sukoshi 少し
a little sukoshi 少し
A.M. gozen 午前
address jushō 住所
adjective keiyōshi 形容詞
adult otona 大人
adverb fukushi 副詞
after sugi 過ぎ
afternoon gogo, hiru 午後，昼
airplane hikōki 飛行機
airport kuko 空港
also -mo も
am dess, imahss です，います
am not de-wa arimasen, imasen ではありません，いません
American (people) Amerika-jin アメリカ人
answer kotae 答え
apple ringo りんご
April Shi-gatsu 四月
are dess, arimahss, imahss です，あります，います
are not arimasen, imasen ありません，いません
arm ude 腕
ashtray haizara 灰皿
at -ni –に
August Hachi-gatsu 八月
autumn aki 秋
back ushiro 後ろ
bad warui 悪い
ball bōru ボール
bank ginkō 銀行
be able dekimahss, dekiru できます，できる
be good at jōzu 上手
be skillful jōzu 上手
be unable dekimasen できません
bean curd tōfu (o-tōfu) 豆腐(お豆腐)
beautiful utsukushii 美しい
beautifully utsukushiku 美しく
became narimashta なりました
become(s) narimahss, naru なります，なる
before mae 前
behind -no ushiro-ni の後ろに
belt beruto ベルト
beside -no soba-ni, -no waki-ni の側に，の脇に
big ōkii 大きい
bird tori 鳥
bloom sakimahss, saku 咲きます，咲く
body karada 体
book hon 本
bookshop hon-ya 本屋
bottom shita 下
box hako 箱
brief case kaban かばん
British, British people Igirisu-jin イギリス人
bullet shinkansen 新幹線
businessman bijinesu-man ビジネスマン
bus stop basutei バス停
by -no waki-ni, -no soba-ni の脇に，の側に
cake kashi (o-kashi) 菓子(お菓子)
call (denwa-o) kamemahss, kakeru (電話を)かけます，かける
came kita, kimashta 来た，来ました
camera kamera カメラ
can dekimahss できます
candy o-kashi お菓子
cannot dekimasen できません
capital Tōkyō 東京
car jidōsha 自動車
cell phone keitai denwa 携帯電話
chair isu 椅子
cheek hoho 頬
chest mune 胸
child, children kodomo 子供
chin ago あご
chopsticks hashi (o-hashi) 箸(お箸)

Chinese, Chinese people Chūgoku-jin 中国人
cigarette tabako たばこ
climate kikō 気候
clock tokei 時計
clothes yōfuku 洋服
cloudy kumori 曇り
coat uwagi 上着
coffee kōhii コーヒー
cold samui, tsumetai 寒い, 冷たい, kaze 風邪, tsumetaku 冷たく
come kimahss, kuru 来ます, 来る
congratulation omedetō-gozaimahss おめでとうございます
cooked rice gohan ご飯
cooking ryōri 料理
cool suzushii, tsumetai 涼しい, 冷たい
correct tadashii 正しい
crisp katai 硬い
cry naku 鳴く
cut (past tense) kirimashta 切りました, kiremahss 切れます
cute kawaii かわいい
daily nichijō 日常
day (date) nichi 日
days of the week yōbi 曜日
December Jūni-gatsu 十二月
delicious oishii おいしい
department sotre depāto デパート
desk tsukue 机
dictionary jisho 辞書
dinnerware shokki 食器
dislike kirai 嫌い
do(es) shimahss, suru します, する
doctor isha 医者
dog inu 犬
doll ningyō 人形
door doa ドア
drawer hikidashi 引き出し
dress yōfuku 洋服
ear(s) mimi 耳
early (adj.) hayai 速い／早い (adv.) hayaku 速く／早く
eating (n.) taberu-koto 食べること
egg tamago たまご
eight hachi, yattsu 八, 八つ
eighth (days of the month) yōka 八日
electric denki 電気
English (language) Eigo 英語
evening ban, yūgata 晩, 夕方
everyday nichijō 日常
Excuse me. Gomen-nasai. ごめんなさい。
exit deguchi 出口
expression hyōgen 表現
eye(s) me 目
eyeglasses megane めがね
face kao 顔
famous yūmei 有名
fast (adj.) hayai 速い／早い; (adv.) hayaku 速く／早く
February Ni-gatsu 二月
feeling gokigen ごきげん
feet ashi 足
fever netsu 熱
field no 野
fifth (day of the month) itsuka 五日
fine ii, yoi, genki いい, 良い, 元気
finger yubi 指
first (day of the month) tsuitachi 一日
fish sakana 魚
five go, itsutsu 五, 五つ
flag hata 旗
flower hana 花
fly/flies tobimahss 飛びます
food tabemono 食べ物
foot ashi 足; (of hill) shita 下
forehead hitai 額
fork fōku フォーク
four yon, shi, yo, yottsu 四, 四つ
fourth (days of the month) yokka 四日
French, French people Furansu-jin フランス人
fresh shinsen 新鮮
Friday Kinyōbi 金曜日
friend tomodachi (o-tomodachi)

友達（お友達）
fruit kudamono くだもの
German, German people Doitsu-jin ドイツ人
give me kudasai ください
go(es) ikimahss (yukimahss), iku (yuku) 行きます, 行く
going (n.) iku-koto (yuku-koto) 行くこと
golf gorufu ゴルフ
good ii, yoi いい, 良い
Good afternoon. Konnichi-wa. こんにちは。
Good day. Konnichi-wa. こんにちは。
Good evening. Komban-wa. こんばんは。
Good morning. Ohayō-gozaimahss. おはようございます。
Good night. Oyasumi-nasai. おやすみなさい。
Goodbye. Sayōnara. さようなら。
greetings aisatsu あいさつ
grew narimashta なりました
grow(s) narimahss, naru なります, なる
beef gyuniku 牛肉
hair kami-no-ke, ke 髪の毛, 毛
half han 半
hand te 手
happi coat happi はっぴ
hard katai 硬い
has/have motte-imahss 持っています
has/have not motte-imasen 持っていません
hat bōshi 帽子
head atama 頭
healthy genki 元気
heavily omoku 重く
heavy omoi 重い
height (of a person) se 背
hello (on the telephone) moshi, moshi もし、もし
hello konnichi-wa こんにちは
here koko, koko-ni ここ, ここに
high (adv.) takaku 高く; (adj.) takai 高い
holiday kyūjitsu 休日
home uchi 家
horizontal yoko 横
hot atsui 暑い/熱い
hotel hoteru ホテル
house uchi 家
how dō, ikaga どう, いかが
how much (numbers) ikutsu いくつ ; (price) ikura いくら
hundred hyaku 百
I wata(ku)shi, wata(ku)shi-wa 私, 私は
I am sorry Gomen-nasai ごめんなさい。
in -ni, -no naka-ni に, の 中に
inside naka, -no naka-ni 中, の 中に
is dess, arimahss, imahss です, あります, います
is not arimasen, imasen ありません, いません
jacket uwagi 上着
January Ichi-gatsu 一月
Japan Nihon 日本
Japanese (dishes) Nihon ryōri 日本料理 ; (language) Nihongo 日本語 ; (people) Nihon-jin 日本人
Japanese rice crackers sembei (o-sembei) せんべい (おせんべい,)
jet plane jettoki ジェット機
July Shichi-gatsu 七月
June Roku-gatsu 六月
knee hiza 膝
large ōkii 大きい
last month sengetsu 先月
last week senshū 先週
late (adj.) osoi 遅い ; (adv.) osoku 遅く
left hidari 左
left side hidari-gawa 左側
leg(s) ashi 足
light (adj.) karui 軽い ; (adv.)

karuku 軽く
lighter raitā ライター
like suki 好き
little chiisai 小さい
long (adj.) nagai 長い; (adv.) nagaku 長く
lovely kawaii かわいい
low (adj.) hikui 低い; (adv.) hikuku 低く
lower part shita 下
luggage nimotsu 荷物
many takusan たくさん
March San-gatsu 三月
May Go-gatsu 五月
meat niku 肉
milk gyūnyū, miruku 牛乳，ミルク
minute fun (pun) 分
Miss -san さん
Monday Getsu-yōbi 月曜日
month tsuki 月
morning asa, gozen 朝，午前
mountain yama 山
mouth kuchi 口
Mr. -san さん
Mrs. -san さん
Mt. Fuji Fujisan 富士山
much takusan たくさん
music ongaku 音楽
my watashi-no 私の
napkin napukin ナプキン
name namae 名前
neck kubi 首
new atarashii 新しい
newspaper shimbun 新聞
next month raigetsu 来月
next to -no soba-ni, -no waki-ni の 側に，の 脇に
next week raishū 来週
nine ku, kyū, kokonotsu 九，九つ
ninth (day of the month) kokonoka 九日
no (interjection) iie いいえ
none sukoshi-mo 少しも
noodles soba そば
noon hiru 昼
nose hana 鼻
November Jūichi-gatsu 十一月
number kazu 数
October Jūgatsu 十月
of -no の
office kaisha 会社
old furui 古い
on -no ue-ni の 上に
one ichi, hitotsu 一，一つ
one person hitori 一人
over -no ue-ni の 上に
o'clock -ji 時
p.m. hiru, gogo 昼，午後
package nimotsu 荷物
painful itai 痛い
pants zubon ズボン
paper kami 紙
part bubun 部分
past (in telling time) sugi 過ぎ
peach momo もも
pearl(s) shinju 真珠
pen pen ペン
pencil empitsu えんぴつ
-people (counting) -nin 人
peppery karai 辛い
personal computer pasokon パソコン
piano piano ピアノ
please kudasai, dōzo ください，どうぞ
please come in irasshaimase いらっしゃいませ
please help yourself dōzo meshiagare, omeshiagari kudasai どうぞ 召し上がれ，お召し上がりください
pork buta-niku ぶた肉
position ichi 位置
postcard hagaki 葉書
pretty kawaii かわいい
quick hayai 速い／早い
quickly hayaku 速く／早く
rain ame 雨
reading (n.) yomu-koto 読むこと
rear ushiro 後ろ
red (adj.) akai 赤い; (adv.) akaku 赤く

restaurant resutoran レストラン
right migi 右 ; tadashii 正しい
road michi 道
rock ishi 石
room heya 部屋
rose bara バラ
round marui 丸い
sake sake 酒
salt shio (o-shio) 塩(お塩)
salty (sio)karai (塩)辛い
sandals zōri 草履
sashimi sashimi 刺身
Saturday Do-yōbi 土曜日
scenery keshiki 景色
season kisetsu 季節
second (day of the month) futsuka 二日
September Kugatsu 九月
seven nana, shichi, nanatsu 七, 七つ
seventh (day of the month) nanoka 七日
shirt shatsu シャツ
shoes kutsu 靴
shop (o-)mise (お)店, -ya −屋
shopping kaimono 買物
short (adj.) hikui 低い ; mijikai 短い; (adv.) mijikaku 短く
shoulder kata 肩
side soba, waki そば, 脇
sing (birds) naku 鳴く
six roku, muttsu 六, 六つ
sixth (day of the month) muika 六日
sky sora 空
slow osoi 遅い
slowly osoku 遅く
small chiisai 小さい
snow yuki 雪
so そう sō
socks kutsushita 靴下
soft yawarakai 柔らかい
sorry sumimasen (suimasen) すみません (すいません)
speaking (n.) hanasu-koto 話すこと
spicy karai 辛い
spoon supūn スプーン
spring haru 春
square shikakui 四角い
state of health gokigen ごきげん
station eki 駅
stockings kutsushita 靴下
stomach o-naka お腹
stone ishi 石
store -ya 屋
street michi 道
student gakusei 学生
study benkyō 勉強
subway station chikatetsu no eki 地下鉄の駅
sugar satō (o-satō) 砂糖 (お砂糖)
suitcase kaban かばん
summer natsu 夏
Sunday Nichi-yōbi 日曜日
supermarket supāmāketto スーパーマーケット
sushi sushi すし
sweet amai 甘い
switch suitchi スイッチ
tail o 尾
tall takai 高い
tasty oishii おいしい
taxi takushii タクシー
tea cha (o-cha) 茶 (お茶)
teacher sensei 先生
teeth ha 歯
telephone denwa 電話
ten jū, tō 十
ten thousand man 万
tenth tōka 十日
thank you arigatō (less formal), arigatō-gozaimahss (more formal) ありがとう, ありがとうございます, sumimasen (suimasen) すみません(すいません)
that ano, sono, are, sore , sore-wa あの, その, あれ, それ, それは
then dewa では
there soko, soko-ni そこ、そこに
there are/is arimahss あります
there are/is not arimasen ありません

third (day of the month) mikka 三日
this kono, kore, kore-wa この，これ，これは
this month kongetsu 今月
this week konshū 今週
thousand sen 千
three san, mittsu 三，三つ
throat nodo のど
Thursday Moku-yōbi 木曜日
ticket kippu 切符
tie nekutai ネクタイ
time -ji 時
to (in telling time) mae, -ni 前，に
to eat taberu-koto 食べること
to go yuku-koto 行くこと
to me watashi-ni 私に
to read yomu-koto 読むこと
to speak hanasu-koto 話すこと
to top of -no ue-ni の 上に
to write kaku-koto 書くこと
to you anata-ni あなたに
today kyō 今日
toe(s) ashi-no-yubi 足の指
tomorrow ashita, asu 明日
tongue shita 舌
too -mo も
tooth ha 歯
toothpick yōji 楊子
top ue 上
train densha 電車
Tuesday Ka-yōbi 火曜日
twentieth (day of the month) hatsuka 二十日
two ni, futatsu 二，二つ
two persons futari 二人
umbrella kasa 傘
under -no shita-ni の 下に
upper part ue 上
vegetable yasai 野菜
vertical tate 縦
very much dōmo どうも
very well jōzu 上手
village sato 里
vocabulary tango 単語
warm atatakai 暖かい/温かい
was/were deshita でした
watch tokei 時計
water mizu (o-mizu) 水（お水）
weather tenki (o-tenki) 天気（お天気）
Wednesday Suiyōbi 水曜日
week shū 週
welcome Irasshaimase いらっしゃいませ
well genki, yoku 元気，良く
well then dewa では
what nani, nan 何
what time nan-ji 何時
where doko どこ
which dore どれ
white shiroi 白い
winter fuyu 冬
wooden clogs geta 下駄
write(s) kakimahss, kaku 書きます，書く
writing (n.) kaku-koto 書くこと
yen en 円
yes hai はい
yesterday kinō 昨日
you anata, anata-wa あなた，あなたは
your anata-no あなたの